Heart & Soul

Heart & Soul

*A Spiritual Course for Meeting
Your Perfect Soulmate*

Rosemary Ellen Guiley, Ph.D.

BERKLEY BOOKS, NEW YORK

A Berkley Book
Published by The Berkley Publishing Group
A division of Penguin Putnam Inc.
375 Hudson Street
New York, New York 10014

This book is an original publication of The Berkley Publishing Group.

Copyright © 2002 by Visionary Living, Inc.
Cover design by Steve Ferlauto.
Text design by Kristin del Rosario.

PRINTING HISTORY
Berkley trade paperback edition/July 2002

Visit our website at
www.penguinputnam.com

Library of Congress Cataloging-in-Publication Data

Guiley, Rosemary.
    Heart and soul : a spiritual course for meeting your perfect soulmate /
Rosemary Ellen Guiley.—Berkley trade pkb. ed.
        p. cm.
    ISBN 0-425-18476-5
    1. Soul mates.   I. Title.

    BF1045.I58 G85 2002
    646.7'7—dc21   2002024683

PRINTED IN THE UNITED STATES OF AMERICA

10 9 8 7 6 5 4 3 2 1

For Yvette and Peter

Contents

Introduction

We all want to be loved, treasured, and cherished, and we want to love, treasure, and cherish someone else in return. We want to have perfect faith and perfect trust in that love—the love of our soulmate, that special person meant just for us.

We have always believed that the perfect love is out there, if we can only find it. We all know people who find their soulmates, and we wonder, why not us? Are soulmates something that happen only to a lucky few?

The answer is, there is a soulmate for each and every one of us! Now, in this lifetime. And there are many things we can do to find that perfect love. I know, because I found mine, and what I learned I am sharing in *Heart and Soul*. I also share the experiences of others.

In this book, you will learn:

• Characteristics of soulmate relationships

- How people meet their soulmates

- How to improve your intuition and spiritual vision

- How to see relationships from spiritual and karmic perspectives

- How to work with the spiritual laws

You *can* have the relationship that will take love to a higher
dimension. The sooner you start, the sooner you can enjoy the
benefits!

The Universe Speaks

There is only one happiness in life, to love and be loved.

—GEORGE SAND

The end of my sixteen-year marriage brought a dramatic change in the landscape of my life. I was in postdivorce blues, and my emotions were on a roller coaster. I was alone and living in a new city, feeling disconnected from everything. I had a hard time concentrating on work. Life as I had known it was over. What would take its place?

I knew I had to pull myself back together. I knew I could do it. I was alone now, but I knew I would love again. My sixteen-year marriage, like all marriages, had its good times and its bad times. It hadn't ended due to any particular cause but from a slow erosion created by a combination of reasons. What I wanted more than anything was to find a new partner with whom I could share a deep and intense love, a connection from the very center of my being. Somewhere out there was my soulmate, and I intended to find him.

As I weathered the emotional bleakness of those days, I didn't know that I was on the verge of a great, sparkling adventure, a journey of magic and mystery, one that would take me around the world and through the very portals of time itself. I was about to discover how to manifest the deepest desires of my heart!

What I learned, you can, too. Do you long for a love that will nourish you and help you flower into the fullest expression of your soul? You can have it! Each and every one of us deserves love, the greatest love we can imagine. For each and every one of us, there is a partner, a soulmate, with whom to share this magnificent love. It is not the stuff of fairy tales and fluffy romances, but real life. Perfect love is part of the divine plan for wholeness and harmony in all the cosmos.

I found my soulmate. You can find yours!

My Journey Begins

That December in the year my divorce became final, I traveled from my home in Maryland out to the West Coast to visit my family for the holidays. My ex and I had once lived in Portland, and we still owned a little beach house on the spectacular Oregon coast. It was my intent to spend some time alone at the cottage for meditation, reflection, and recharging my inner batteries.

In making my travel plans, I saw that the full moon in December would occur at the end of the month—a perfect time to be at the beach. I'm a Cancer, a Moon Child, and I've always felt a special, mystical kinship with the moon. When I was a child, I gazed at the full moon through a little telescope and was so awestruck at its magnified majesty that I decided then and there to be an astronomer when I grew up. Life took another course—into writing—but for many years I was an active and enthusiastic amateur astronomer. I've also appreciated the mythology and folklore around the moon, and I have always paid attention to its phases.

The moon is ruled by the divine feminine aspect of God, or Goddess. It governs the tides, moods, the rhythms of life, and the great mysteries of life. A full moon at my private beach retreat seemed like the ideal setting to contemplate my crossroads of life.

This interest in the moon and mythology is part of my over-all work in realms of the esoteric and mystical. Initially, my work as a writer took me into the paranormal, and then into the mys-tical—the exploration of the relationship of the soul to God. Besides mysticism, I have delved into the ancient mystery teach-ings, the esoteric science of transformation called alchemy, dreams, healing, prayer, meditation, reincarnation, angels, ghosts, survival after death, and more. My varied and wide-ranging background was to prove valuable in my discoveries of how to create reality and bring dreams into being.

After the holidays, I traveled down to Portland and picked up my longtime soulmate friend, Sue. Together we drove to the coast to the little town of Manzanita, named for a seacoast tree common to the area. It was late on a cold but sunny afternoon when we arrived at The Mumbles, the name of my cottage. The Mumbles was christened after a charming town by the same name on the southern coast of Wales, where the great poet Dylan Thomas once held forth in smoky pubs. My ex and I had named the cottage in reminder of fond memories of Wales. Like The Mumbles of Wales, Manzanita was quaint and often under a drizzle.

We dropped off our gear and ran straight down the hill to the beach for a walk before sunset. I never failed to be stunned by the grand vista of the coast. Oregon beaches have a raw and wild beauty. The surf is rough and the weather cool and damp, even in the summer. The beaches are packed gray sand—some are quite rocky—and are not the soft sunbathing havens found farther south in California. I have always preferred the raw and wild to the sunbathing shore.

The Manzanita beach is a great walking beach. To the north, the beach is short and ends in a cove created by a mountain on the edge of the sea. To the south, the beach stretches for miles and miles until it disappears on the horizon. To the west is the vast blue gray expanse of Pacific Ocean. To the east are the emerald, wooded peaks of the coastal mountain range. The surf rolls in with a continuous, eternal roar. The beach can absorb many people and still seem empty. Set against the grand scale of nature, one feels quite small here, yet part of the cosmic picture.

Sue and I set off down the beach, a cool wind at our backs. The curling, roaring surf glistened in the sunlight. Circling gulls cried overhead. Bands of sanderlings scurried about, pecking into the sand for their last meal of the day. The air was fresh with salt.

One of the things that I have always liked about the beach is that it immediately washes away any stress and worries. That's how I felt now—simply at peace and at one with my surroundings. I was especially happy to arrive in plenty of time for the sunset, which often is spectacular. Clouds that are spread out over the great canopy of sky light up in huge washes of roses, oranges, pinks, and reds that linger long into the darkening indigo of sky.

I looked at the sun, a fiery orange globe poised over the endless sea. I turned the other way and saw rising over the rounded mountains the ghostly globe of the full moon. I was struck by the symmetry. It seemed that in that instant the cosmic rulers of the day and night were in perfect balance, each the same distance above the horizon: the sun dying to the day and the moon birthing to the night, neither one having supremacy over the other. Sun and moon, day and night, light and dark, masculine and feminine—the balance and harmony of all the opposites of the cosmos were suddenly expressed in this exquisite vision.

Suddenly I was swept up into a strange but thrilling feeling. It seemed as though a door of time opened, and I was thrust into the Eternal Now, where all things are in perfect balance. I saw that I was part of that balance, and thus my life, with all my experiences, longings, actions, and goals, was part of that balance, too.

Caught in this timelessness, I felt that whatever I wished for now would come to pass. I was in total harmony with the flow of the universe. Whatever forces I set in motion would not go amiss.

Quickly I made three wishes. I put all the energy, will, and intensity into them that I could muster, as though every cell of my being was mobilized in support of them. I then thanked the Creator, or God/Goddess/All That Is, for the blessings to follow. I asked the universe for signs: "If this be so, then please give me signs."

And then the moment was over. I was out of the timelessness, back on the Manzanita beach, watching the sun sink into the sea and the full moon gain brilliance in the darkening sky.

But I was changed. A peculiar electricity tingled through me.

Quite unexpectedly, I had experienced something out of the ordinary—a mystical state of being in which I encountered something greater than myself, but of which I was a vital part. Some psychologists call this a *peak experience,* a moment in which we are infused with a transcendent joy, a union with nature, and a sense of tremendous potential. We all have at least a few such experiences throughout life. Typically, they come when we are out in nature, feeling good, and not preoccupied in thought. For many, they are moments filled with inspiration, creativity, and even genius.

Although this happened to me spontaneously, I later discovered that we can consciously create such moments so that we can better shape our destiny: for love, for fulfillment, for success, for prosperity. I learned how to do it, and I will show you how to do it, too.

The idea of making wishes had occurred to me as spontaneously as the experience itself. They carried an energy, a force, to them. It wasn't the same as casual wishes I'd made over falling stars and the like. Somehow, these were different. Still, I wondered if, and how, the wishes would come to pass.

After a couple of days, Sue departed and left me to my solitude. I lived according to my natural rhythms, not by the clock. I ate when I was hungry, went to bed when I was tired, arose when I was refreshed. I made cozy fires in the freestanding fireplace in The Mumbles, and curled up with books and pots of herbal tea. I meditated and daydreamed.

I roamed the beach by day and by night. At night, under the glow of the moon and the canopy of shimmering stars, the beach takes on a new personality. The spectral, white surf and the mist that rises after dark make the entire landscape seem otherworldly.

Spirits dance on the waves—the nymphs of Neptune singing to the breaking of the sea on the shore. The night is a vault of secrets and mystery. On this trip, I did not feel like an observer of the mystery but rather a participant in the mystery.

The Signs Appear

It was after I was alone that I received the signs I'd requested.

It has always been my habit at the beach to do casual beachcombing. I don't rivet my gaze to the sand, but if something catches the corner of my eye, I stop and investigate. The Oregon beach has never been a beachcomber's paradise, however. The rough surf breaks up most of what washes in on the tides. One does find a bounty of whole but plain-looking mussel shells, limpets, and tiny clamshells. Unusual shells are rare. So are whole sand dollars, which litter the beach in shards.

One morning I was out in the chilly gray hours of dawn. The beach was a landscape of wet sand, tide pools, and wisps of fog. As I walked along, my eye was drawn to a stone. It was gray and didn't particularly stand out from the sand. I'm not one to collect many stones, but for some reason, this one beckoned to me.

I picked it up and was excited to see that it was a heart-shaped stone. On one side was a crisscross of lines meeting at the center. It reminded me of the lines of destiny on the palm of a hand. I felt it tingle as I held it. I knew this was the sign for my first wish. I asked the angels of nature for permission to keep it and put the stone in my pocket.

The next day I received my second sign. A whole sand dollar! I couldn't believe it. In all the years that I had been going to the Oregon coast, I had never found a whole one. Gingerly I turned it over, half expecting it to disintegrate at my touch. Not a nick or fracture was on it. I took it back to The Mumbles and added it to the heart-shaped stone.

On the following day, the third sign arrived. It was something I'd never seen the likes of at this beach—a whole snail shell, red in color with a band of white running horizontally around it. It was beautiful and highly significant to me. I tried to find other shells like it, for sometimes batches of things wash in at once, but found none. This mysterious, red and white shell was definitely my third sign.

So now I had three signs for my three wishes. I was elated! The universe had clearly spoken; forces were in motion.

But it didn't stop there. On the next day, my last at the beach, I received two more signs: another whole sand dollar and a large, intact clamshell big enough to hold all of my treasures. It was as though the universe were giving me a bonus and a high sign. I felt doubly blessed because all of the signs were gifts of the seashore, which is ruled by the tides. The tides are ruled by the moon. The moon is ruled by Goddess. Goddess is the giver of bounty.

The numbers involved in this experience also had significance. In the ancient mystery traditions of esoteric wisdom, numbers carry their own unique vibrations that have a relation to the cosmic picture.

I made three wishes. In esoteric lore, three is the magical number that opens the gateways to other realms. It is the number of creation. This is why, for example, things are done in threes in stories of folklore throughout the world: three wishes, three spells, three charms, three chances, and so on.

My first wish was to be connected to my soulmate. In answer, I received the heart-shaped stone with lines of destiny meeting right in the center—the core of being.

My second wish was for better financial prosperity. What better reply from the realm of the sea than a whole sand dollar, a symbol of plenty?

My third wish was for improved health. Fortunately, I have never suffered from great health problems. I wished for overall good health, but I specifically wanted to rid myself of a tendency to be stricken with frequent respiratory infections that were rather debilitating. The red and white of the snail shell held the answer. The shell protects the body of the snail. Red is the color of vitality. White symbolizes the spiritual. Thus I could see the sign pointing to an improvement in vitality and protection of health. The red and white also alluded to the soulmate wish as well. In alchemy, red symbolizes the masculine and white symbolizes the feminine. The two were united on the shell, which itself is a symbol of Goddess and therefore rebirth.

Then I was given two more signs: another sand dollar and another shell, bringing the total to five. This increased the significance of all the signs. The second sand dollar emphasized not only prosperity, but lots of it. The clamshell, because of its shape and size, neatly wrapped everything into a package as a container. Most significantly, five is the number of change, especially concerning spiritual matters. Thus, my five signs were a signal that changes in my life pertaining to my wishes were indeed in the works and would involve me on a spiritual level.

In happy spirits, I said good-bye to the sea and the beach and returned to the suburbs of Baltimore, my new home after many years in New York and Connecticut. I put my treasures in a little box with a trumpeting angel on the cover. The angel seemed to be heralding something new. *I'm all for that!* I thought.

In the ensuing weeks, I became engrossed in matters of daily life: renewing my work, building a new social life, paying the bills, staying in shape. The pleasant experience of the beach faded into the background. I let the energy of the universe, set in motion, take its proper course.

The forces of the universe moved swiftly. About seven weeks after my mystical experience at Manzanita, my first wish appeared. His name was Tom.

2

The Bridge to Heaven

When two souls have finally found each other there is
established between them a union which begins on earth
and continues forever in heaven.

— Victor Hugo

Tom arrived when I was least expecting him. In fact, that's often the way it works. Like the watched pot that doesn't boil, the soulmate quest that is too consuming is slow to produce results.

One Friday night in the February following my beach experience, I attended the monthly meeting of a metaphysically oriented group in Baltimore. I had never attended before, and I met up with two female friends. Although I have numerous metaphysical interests and hoped to find a man who shared those interests, I did not necessarily expect to meet my soulmate at one of the many such meetings I attended for professional and personal reasons. Why? Most of the attendees are usually women (who are solo or who have uninterested partners), or couples.

The beauty of the search for love is that you never know when the magic moment will happen. As I slipped in the door late and found an empty chair in the crowded room, I had no idea that lightning was about to strike. I was noticed by a man who was new to the group—and who was single again like me and also searching for his ideal mate.

At the end of the meeting, he materialized in front of me to introduce himself. I found myself looking up into a handsome, boyish face and blue eyes that radiated a sunny and magnetic energy. An electric thrill ran through me, and I was overtaken by a feeling that *something big* was about to begin. Tom was feeling the same thing. It was a magic moment for both of us. We took a deep breath and let ourselves go into that giddy free fall of love at first sight.

Not that the music swelled and we dashed into each other's arms with cries of "I've been waiting all my life for you!" No. This was a meeting of two Cancerians—Tom is a double Cancer—and the crabs of the zodiac are famous for their caution. The romantic, right-brain giddiness that swept over me was immediately countered with a stern, left-brain inner voice that said, *Hold on, now, let's not get carried away. He's probably got scads of girlfriends!* He didn't, however—not a single one. Tom was not interested in casual relationships; he had his radar out for "the one."

After that meeting, it took Tom awhile to ask me out, much to my chagrin. I thought perhaps I'd imagined the whole thing, but it was just the cautious crab in him, working through things on his end. Tom told me later that he knew right from the start that the relationship would be big. When he made the phone call, he knew what it would initiate.

We quickly discovered that we shared mutual interests, outlooks, dreams and visions—not to mention a great physical attraction! What was more, this romance had a special freshness that I hadn't experienced in a long time. I felt like a teenager in love for the very first time.

That feeling is a hallmark of many soulmate relationships. It doesn't matter how old you are or how many times you've been in and out of love; when your soulmate appears, it wipes the slate clean. You love as though you have never loved before.

Every time I talked to Tom, every time I saw him, I was awash in this feeling of love for the first time. We were both totally smitten with each other, and yet each of us moved with caution, careful not to show too much but to play it as cool as we could. We didn't succeed much in fooling each other! We were hampered somewhat by the fact that we lived nearly sixty miles apart and also by travel schedules that had one of us coming while the other was going.

By our second date, I knew we would marry. I just *knew* it, deep inside. That left-brain voice kept saying, *What's the rush? You hardly know him!* But I did know him, in a way that transcended words. I knew he was the soulmate I'd longed for. My friends had to endure my starry-eyed rapture.

On our second date, we got in Tom's car, and the radio came on when he started the ignition. The station tuned in was playing an old Simon & Garfunkel hit, "Scarborough Fair." "There's that song again!" Tom exclaimed. He went on to tell me that since meeting me, he was hearing the song everywhere. It was on the radio nearly every time he turned it on. Friends sang it. He even caught himself singing it in the shower one morning. It kept running through his mind.

Now, "Scarborough Fair" is not one of those golden oldies that one hears with great frequency on the radio. But for us, it had importance because of the refrain line that refers to the herb rosemary. The fact that Tom was hearing this song a lot meant one thing: synchronicity, or *meaningful coincidence*. It was the universe speaking: pay attention! I had to laugh.

Despite our intense mutual physical attraction, we did not dash to the bedroom. Part of it was common sense and part of it was, as before, Cancerian caution. But there was also a feeling that this was so special, so sacred, the relationship needed to be nurtured and savored, and not spoiled by premature sex. We kissed on our second date. Such a thunder of emotion went into it that I could barely sleep all night. And Tom was so dazzled that he spent several hours trying to get home. First he drove north on the freeway instead of south, and then he realized after a while that he was driving around the Baltimore beltway in the wrong direction.

Our travel schedules were taking us both overseas during the summer. Tom was going to Paris on a job assignment, and I was going to England, Scotland, and the Isle of Man. "Why don't you come to Paris?" Tom said. He didn't have to ask twice.

Messages in the Land of the Nature Gods

I celebrated the summer solstice with friends at Findhorn, located far north in Scotland on the Moray Firth, or sea. Findhorn is the legendary spiritual city of light made famous by its founders' contact with the nature spirits, or devas. Findhorn the spiritual community (there is also a village of Findhorn) was founded in the 1960s. Founders Peter and Eileen Caddy and Dorothy McLean received daily guidance from the devas, enabling them to have a flourishing garden in poor, sandy soil.

They were inspired to build a community based on love, coop-
eration, and manifestation. The community swelled to hundreds,
and for a time boasted the presence of mystic David Spangler
from America. Findhorn became an international mecca for
spiritual pilgrims.

Of the original founders, only Eileen remains. McLean left in
1973, and Peter left in 1979. He was killed in an automobile accident in 1994. Findhorn still attracts pilgrims, people who want
to visit or take up residence or attend one of the many programs
offered.

Because of its latitude, Findhorn is nearly a land of the mid-
night sun at the solstice and hosts a traditional Celtic Midsummer Festival. It sounded magical, and so I had made plans
months earlier to attend.

By the time I arrived, I seemed to be in a constant slipstream
of magic, and there was plenty of it at Findhorn. A wild and
primitive atmosphere still envelops the landscape, and those who
seek contact with the nature spirits—and are pure of heart in
their intent—are often rewarded. I took frequent hikes to the
beach, winding first through trees and then through thickets of
gorse, a scrubby brush that grows in the sandy soil. I felt in harmony with the place. Late in the evenings when twilight took
over, I could shift my consciousness and perceive the glow of
nature spirits, shining like points of fairy lights.

It is said that if the nature gods approve of you, Pan himself—the king of the nature spirits—might grace your presence. One day when I was hiking alone to the beach, I
suddenly heard the distinct sound of panpipes, Pan's musical
flute, behind me. Thinking first that someone from the village
was coming up behind me, I turned, but the trail was empty. I

had no human company. I resumed walking. The soft music, faint at times, accompanied me until I was out of the gorse and on to open sand.

I mention these experiences because they were products of the inner harmony I felt with my environment. Establishing harmony is a key element in manifesting what we desire. It is difficult to orchestrate the energies of the universe if we are not in the flow.

Prior to my departure, I had asked Tom for a photograph of him to take along with me. I carried it in my wallet and took it out every night to prop up by my bedside. Something strange began to happen. Every time I looked at the photo, I saw a vision superimposed over it—a vision of our wedding, complete with details of the rings on our fingers. We hadn't yet mentioned the *M* word, or even the *L* word, *love,* but I knew with a certainty that consumed my being that we would be married soon, and that it was the right course of action. Every night I said to the photo, "Tom, I love you, and I'm going to marry you!" I resolved then to let events in linear time catch up with something that I knew was already a reality.

While staying at Findhorn, I went through my little ritual every night, feeling an added boost from the mystery of the place. Findhorn residents had long prided themselves on their ability to manifest whatever they needed by being in harmony with the universe. Now here I was, manifesting my destiny with my soulmate with my prayers, meditation, affirmations, and visions.

The night of Midsummer Eve, ushering in the longest day of the year, seemed especially potent with spiritual power, reminiscent of my stay at the beach at Manzanita. After feasting and maypole dancing, we celebrants hiked down to the stony beach for an all-night bonfire and Celtic storytelling. The sun went down over the water around eleven P.M. The sky, however, never grew completely dark but remained a spooky gray twilight. A yellow orange glow lingered over the water where the sun had vanished. Shortly, a pink glow appeared far in the northeast, announcing the rising of the sun that would occur in a few short hours. Both glow of sunset and sunrise hung in the sky. A full moon shone through ever-shifting clouds, making a marriage of solar and lunar energies. The unseen of the nature kingdom were everywhere. I knew the sun would never set on my relationship with Tom. I said my prayers for guidance, love, and happiness.

In a few days, I was on a plane to Paris.

Realizing the Vision

I was very nervous. That kid-in-love-for-the-first-time feeling overwhelmed me. I would be sharing a hotel room with Tom, and that meant a consummation of the relationship—an irrevocable commitment. I literally felt like a virgin bride. It made me feel silly at times, but it was undeniable. There was a distinct, never-before essence to this relationship!

Tom met me at the airport. Paris was hot, steamy, and jammed with tourists. I barely noticed. I was in a dream—in one of the most romantic cities on Earth, in the summertime, with my soulmate.

We strolled the streets, lunched at a café (I couldn't taste the food), and tried to be nonchalant about it all. Both of us were secretly nervous about what was to come.

We dined late at a cozy, candlelit cellar on the Île de la Cité. Afterward, we walked along the Seine, arm in arm. The streets were full of people, enjoying the warm night with its long twilight. Street musicians serenaded the crowds. Paris is the city of lovers, and it seemed that pairs of lovers were everywhere. Above, a golden moon, full at the solstice but still ripe in body, rode high in the sky, casting a spell of magic.

We found a place to sit by the river and got lost in each other. "You know, Rosemary," Tom said, looking into my eyes, "I love you." I felt the universe expand into a timeless space. "I love *you*," I said. I wanted the moment to last forever, for this summer night in Paris when the world changed to be suspended in a drop of amber.

The best was to come, in the total union of body, mind, and soul.

We joined households that fall and began planning our marriage.

Tom asked me what sort of ring I would like. That was easy! I knew I would have the one I saw in my vision. Then Tom surprised me by saying he didn't think he wanted a ring. He had never been in the habit of wearing jewelry—it had even been discouraged by his previous religion, and he had not worn a wedding ring in his prior marriage. That threw me for a loop. In my vision, he was clearly wearing a wedding ring. I hadn't described the vision, so I let it ride. But just before we went shopping to pick out my ring, Tom announced that he would like a wedding ring after all. This relationship was special and different, and a wedding ring would be an important symbol of the bond between us, he explained.

The ring he selected was just like the one in my vision.

The Bridge to Heaven

We set a wedding date and time by astrology, using the horoscope of our partnership—the combination of each of our natal horoscopes. What we sought was a heavenly configuration that bestowed positive energies upon the union.

Fortunately, we did not have to get married in the middle of the night in order to obtain a favorable astrological setting! The date was set for Friday, May 5, 1995. We wanted the ceremony to be completed by 7:30 P.M., and so we worked backward in planning what would happen when.

We opted for a very small and private ceremony, surrounded by a handful of family and friends. We wrote our own ceremony and vows. Our dear friend, the author and Reverend Jayne Howard-Feldman, known as the Angel Lady for her work with the angelic kingdom, officiated. We were further blessed with Jayne's generous sharing of her delightful country house, Angel Heights, in the rolling farmlands north of Baltimore. We were married beneath a giant oak tree, looking out over a velvety landscape fresh with budding trees and flowers that stretched for miles and miles. Geese flew overhead, and birds twittered in the trees. Squirrels and rabbits browsed nearby in the brush. The lengthening rays of the setting sun in the west gave pink and orange color to the cloud-graced sky.

The ceremony went smoothly, and we were pronounced

husband and wife at the desired time. Just as our little group broke to begin throwing rose petals, someone shouted and pointed to the sky. I looked to the east. There, framed against gray, moisture-laden clouds, was a double rainbow, two glorious arcs of color, one atop the other. The rainbow has tremendous spiritual and mystical significance. It is the bridge to heaven and a symbol of God's covenant with humanity. It shows the way to the treasures of the heart. It is good luck and prosperity. Our union was being blessed by the gods, not just once, but twice. The angels were singing. I burst into tears of joy. I couldn't ask for a more auspicious beginning.

It may seem that the relationship was all stardust, and that we were lost in rose-colored glamour. Far from it. Underneath the romance and glitter was the real-life practicality of establishing a marriage.

As time goes on, the relationship has become richer, a source of great nourishment, strength, and love. No relationship is ever problem free, however, but a soulmate relationship has its own special ease and harmony, for the soul vibrations of the two persons involved merge together with great compatibility. Soulmates abide in love, trust, and faith, not only with each other but with the greater whole of all that is—with the universe and with God.

What I learned about manifestation did not end here. There is more to soulmates than finding one. The real challenge lies in manifesting an ongoing relationship that retains its zest, passion, commitment, and support. To do that we must be able to envision our highest and greatest potential and reach inside for the ability to realize it. We must *live* in the fullest sense of the word.

About my other two wishes made on the beach: they came true, too. Within a few months, both my prosperity and my health began a steady improvement. I am now blessed in all ways, but most importantly, in love.

3
What Is a Soulmate?

Harmony is pure love, for love is complete agreement.

—LOPE DE VEGA

A popular notion about soulmates is that there is one person, and one person only, who is our ideal and perfect partner. If we find that person, we remain forever in a state of intense passion and bliss.

Actually, there are many kinds of soulmate relationships, and we have more than one in a lifetime. Some of us may have one romantic soulmate; others may have two or more.

In addition to romantic soulmate relationships, we have soulmate bonds with family and friends.

Soulmate relationships are harmonious and happy, but even in the best of them, conflicts arise. Soulmates have differences and problems, but the differences seldom put an end to the relationship.

A soulmate relationship is one that fosters a deep love and happiness and promotes spiritual growth for both partners. The two souls often feel they have shared significant relationships in past lives. We can find a soulmate at any time in life.

Twin Souls

Our ideas about soulmates are shaped by the great Greek philosophers. Plato, quoting Aristophanes, wrote in his work *Symposium* about twin souls. In the beginning, souls were complete, with two persons residing in a body. Their wholeness made them very powerful. Zeus, the dominant god, was fearful of this power. So he split each soul in two. Ever since then, souls have searched the earth for their other half. When one meets his or her other half, the two are "lost in an amazement of love and friendship and intimacy and one will not be out of the other's sight for even a moment," said Aristophanes.

The twin soul is one kind of soulmate relationship. It comes in a romantic partner with whom we feel truly complete. It's the person who seems to be our missing half, who makes us whole. We share a passion of body, mind, and spirit. John Lennon expressed this sentiment about Yoko Ono, for whom he left his first wife, Cynthia. He described himself and Yoko as "two halves and now we are whole." There certainly was a great passion between them, and their bonding stimulated a tremendous outflowing of creativity. But there was also great conflict.

Twin soul relationships are likely to last until death. The partners simply cannot and do not want to be without each other, no matter what stresses arise. Paul McCartney described his wife, Linda, as his soulmate and best friend: "the love of my life." In twenty-nine years of marriage, the two spent only nine nights apart, when Paul was arrested and jailed in Japan in 1980 for possession of marijuana. "I am privileged to have been her lover for thirty years," Paul said upon Linda's death from cancer in April 1998. "In all that time, except for one enforced absence, we never spent a single night apart. When people asked why, we would say, 'What for?' " One of Paul's aides and friends, Geoff Baker, told the media that it was difficult for Paul to put his grief into words "because they were the ultimate soulmates. Throughout their married life they were each other's twin. No couple—in fact no mum and dad and their four children—could ever have been closer." Paul paid continuing tribute to their union in the dozens of love songs he wrote to Linda over the years.

Poets Elizabeth Barrett and Robert Browning are another example of twin souls. They found each other through the oddest of circumstances and defied family opposition to marry and be together. Elizabeth was an invalid, confined to her room not only by her health but by a domineering father who forbade any of his children to marry. Her poetry nonetheless circulated in the outside world and made her famous. In 1845, the up-and-coming poet Robert Browning wrote her an admiring letter in which he boldly declared his love for both her work and for her, even though they had never met. She answered him the next day. He begged to see her, but she declined.

A correspondence ensued, and through the energy of the written word, they recognized each other at the soul level. Elizabeth and Robert fell in love by letter—574 of them, written over twenty months. Five months after their first letters, they finally met, but by then their hearts and souls were already entwined. Elizabeth found Robert to be her "ideal man, fleshed out."

Infused by Robert's love, Elizabeth blossomed and regained health. They married secretly and left England to live in Italy. They had a son. They stimulated each other creatively. The famous line, "How do I love thee? Let me count the ways," was penned by Elizabeth in her collection *Sonnets from the Portuguese* as a love tribute to Robert. The full poem stands as one of the most graceful expressions of soulmate love:

> *How do I love thee? Let me count the ways.*
> *I love thee to the depth and breadth and height*
> *My soul can reach, when feeling out of sight*
> *For the ends of Being and ideal Grace.*
> *I love thee to the level of every day's*
> *Most quiet need, by sun and candle-light.*
> *I love thee freely, as men strive for right;*
> *I love thee purely, as they turn from praise.*
> *I love thee with the passion put to use*
> *In my old griefs, and with my childhood's faith.*
> *I love thee with a love I seemed to lose*
> *With my lost saints—I love thee with the breath,*
> *Smiles, tears, of all my life!—and, if God choose,*
> *I shall but love thee better after death.*

Elizabeth, who was older than Robert, died in his arms in 1861. Robert remained a widower until his own death twenty-eight years later. Attractive women pursued him, but they held no interest for him. He declared that his heart had gone to the grave with Elizabeth.

Soul Groups

Each of us shares affinities with other souls that draw us together again and again across time. Soulmates often recognize each other from the same soul group.

In the Western mystery tradition, God, or the Oneness, created the descent of the spiritual into the material by subdividing the One into the many. The spiritual path of all of us, regardless of our soul groups, is to return to the One.

Through this subdivision, there are clusters of souls who share certain things in common, such as an ethnic, karmic, cultural, or spiritual purpose that evolves over a series of lifetimes. Members of the group may choose to reincarnate at the same time to share more experiences together and to further their common soul evolution. Bonding deepens as lifetimes are layered upon lifetimes. Such soulmate relationships may take the form of romantic partnerships, family ties, or deep friendships. We all meet people who seem very familiar to us, like we have known them for a long time or from some time lost in the distant past. Such people may be part of our soul group. They are truly our soulmates.

According to the seer Edgar Cayce, souls have reincarnated in groups throughout history. The largest group comprises the planet itself, for earth is not the only place in the cosmos to live. Soul groups are fluid, their ranks constantly shifting as individual souls change course. In the thousands of Cayce readings, two major soul groups were identified: Group 1 includes souls who lived in early Atlantis, early ancient Egypt, Persia during the time of Croesus I and Croesus II, Palestine, the Crusades, and

Colonial America. Group 2 includes souls who lived in late Atlantis, late ancient Egypt, early Greece, Rome during the time of Christ, France during the time of Louis XIV, XV, and XVI, and the American Civil War.

The souls who lived during the times in these two groups also most likely had other lives; these periods were ones of great importance in the course of human events and evolution. In their reincarnations, soul groups are subject to karma and planetary influences. A particular group may not desire to collectively reincarnate, for example, but be required to do so for the purposes of balancing karma. Some members of soul groups may be present in a particular cycle in spirit form, as guides, rather than in the flesh, and still have an influence upon earthly affairs.

There are many smaller groups of souls, and subgroups within groups.

Cayce died on January 3, 1945, shortly before the end of World War II, another great period of world trauma and change. Other watershed periods will produce new soul groups or cycles of groups.

Author and past-life regressionist Dick Sutphen said in the 1970s that he discovered a soul group of 25,000 who had lived 1,400 years ago in Teotihuacan in central Mexico. A religious, cultural, economic, and political center, its population may have reached a peak of 200,000. It was twelve square miles in size, larger than the area contained within the walls of Imperial Rome under the caesars, a contemporary civilization. By the time the Aztecs arrived in 1325 A.D., it was long deserted and in ruins. The Aztecs named the place Teotihuacan, which means "the place where men become gods."

In 1974, Sutphen and his wife, Tara, visited Teotihuacan and walked among the ruins, including the Street of the Dead, mounds in which the Aztecs believed were buried the gods. Sutphen felt a sense of déjà vu. He experienced a dream in which he was in ancient Teotihuacan. Thousands of persons filled the street and night. Elegantly robed men lined the steps of the Pyramid of the Moon, atop which was lit a huge fire. In the dream, he was instructed to "get the books together."

According to the information that unfolded over time, Sutphen and Tara felt they had been part of a group of 25,000 persons who had made a pact to reincarnate every 700 years to present the spiritual knowledge that they had possessed at that time.

In *A Tribe Returned,* author and past-life regressionist Janet Cunningham chronicles the discovery of twenty-five persons, including herself and her husband, that had belonged together in a Native American tribe. Most of the tribe had been massacred by whites. In their present lives, the twenty-five souls were drawn together in family, friends, and acquaintances. The remembering and sharing of their past-life memories led to healing and a liberation of spirit.

Similarly, Rabbi Yonassan Gershom has helped members of another soul group, Jewish victims of the Holocaust, reconnect in present lives. His books *Beyond the Ashes* and *From Ashes to Healing* explore those stories.

Karmic Soulmate Ties

We create karmic affinities from all of our relationships in a lifetime. Whenever we form a relationship with another soul, cords of the universal energy are sent out. The life energy is the universal substance that connects and nourishes all things, and which goes by different names such as *prana, chi, ki, mana,* and so on. These cords of energy connect us through the chakras, major interfaces in our auric envelope that allow the universal life force to penetrate our being and body for our nourishment. The cords can remain even when a relationship comes to an end. Relationships that are intense or long lasting build up powerful cords of energy that resonate across time. If relationships are short or mild, the cords of energy are much weaker. If relationships are not renewed in other lifetimes, the cords wither. If they do not break, they can be reactivated by the right set of karmic circumstances.

The cords of life energy reach out and draw to us specific souls. In any lifetime, we meet up with people for the purposes of karmic balancing. Perhaps we need to redress wrongs, or we owe a debt of gratitude or service. When the balancing is complete, the relationship ends. If the relationship ends without balance, the karma is left for another opportunity, perhaps in another life.

Relationships intended to balance karma can be intense, even turbulent. We feel an overwhelming attraction to someone, but the relationship lacks harmony.

History is full of great love relationships that were fraught with trouble and ended in tragedy. The pattern is always the same: two persons are inexorably, fatally, drawn to each other like moths to a flame. But instead of love and harmony, their relationship creates great pain and suffering.

Consider the case of Heloise and Abelard, who lived in Europe during the twelfth century. Abelard, the son of a Brittany knight, was a famous theologian and teacher who held the chair of philosophy and theology at Notre-Dame. At the peak of his teaching career, he met Heloise, a teenager nearly twenty years his junior. Smitten with her, he arranged to be hired as her private tutor and live in her uncle's house where she resided. He was glamorous; she was vulnerable. He seduced her. Her love for him became an obsession, and she surrendered her will to him. Abelard lost interest in his work.

The affair created a great scandal. Heloise became pregnant and bore an illegitimate son. She and Abelard were secretly married. But her uncle, enraged at the disgrace brought to his family, had Abelard attacked and castrated.

Shattered, Abelard decided to retire to a monastery. He forced Heloise to enter a convent. The two of them were miserable for the rest of their lives. They never saw each other again, but they did communicate by letter.

"Of all wretched women I am the most wretched, and amongst the unhappy I am unhappiest," Heloise wrote to Abelard. "The higher I was exalted when you preferred me to all women, the greater my suffering over my own fall and yours, when I was flung down; for the higher the ascent, the heavier the fall."

The intense attraction between these two souls indicates that a karmic balancing was in order. But it never took place. Their shipwreck upon the rocks of obsession and control probably created an even greater karmic debt between the two.

Is such a relationship redeemable? Can it ever become a happy union? Yes, over time. As they evolve and work out the karma, both souls may agree to come together again in a higher and more supportive relationship.

Sometimes karmic balancing is very harmonious, such as when two souls meet up to support, love, and nurture each other. For fifteen years, Erin and Mark enjoyed a close marriage. Their friends called them "soulmates" and "made for each other." Friends and family were shocked and mystified when the marriage came to an end. The parting was painful for both Erin and Mark. When Erin was able to assess the relationship in retrospect, she described it as a spiritual contract. They had come together to help each other get a footing in life. Then they arrived at a point where what had brought them together seemed completed. It became necessary to move on in separate directions.

Through past-life recall, Erin saw that she and Mark had been there for each other in various lifetimes. It was indeed a soulmate connection, one that focused on helping one or the other spread the wings of self-confidence and independence. In the lifetime before this, Erin had experienced great difficulties and setbacks. She felt in need of a break. During the time between lives, the oversouls of herself and Mark had set an intent to find each other in the next life and steady the ship.

Sometimes the karmic balancing between souls is stressful. Perhaps one soul has a debt to another. Perhaps one soul remains bent on exacting revenge for a past-life grievance. Ideally, we meet up with certain souls to forgive, release, and love, but that does not always prove to be the case. Every soul grows at its own pace, and sometimes it takes us awhile to learn our cosmic lessons.

Karmic balancing sets up some powerful attractions. Sometimes we mistake the attraction for soulmate compatibility. When Linda met the man she felt was her soulmate, it seemed like the perfect union. He was considerate and caring, and the two of them fit together like hand and glove. She felt as though she could share the deepest parts of herself with Rick with no fear.

But after she surrendered completely into the relationship, the tenor of it began to change. Rick began an emotional withdrawal. He became more demanding, even manipulative. Linda found herself giving up friendships and interests that displeased him. Soon she was completely dependent upon Rick for approval and support. Then suddenly he abandoned her without warning.

Linda was devastated, and it took a long time for her to repair her emotional wounds. She wondered why she had been so wrong. How could she have seen Rick as a soulmate when he hurt her so badly? What had she done wrong? Her confidence in her judgment and in herself was badly shaken. She was afraid to become involved with anyone again.

Linda came to me for an intuitive reading to try to find the answers to her questions about where and why things went so wrong. I suggested that she might find the answers in past lives, and so we took a time journey.

I could see many cords of energy between Rick and Linda that involved multiple lifetimes together. They had shared strong romantic and friendship relationships. Linda glimpsed several lifetimes in which the same pattern of control and abandonment were repeated. There were powerful attractions between the two. Rick had become fascinated with using his personal power to control others. When he succeeded, the challenge was gone, and so he moved on. Linda kept hoping she could redeem him. And so the pattern went.

Realizing this brought a profound healing to Linda. Things hadn't gone wrong because of her own inadequacies.

After returning from the time journey, I asked Linda what course of action she wanted to take as a result of what she had learned. She said that she wanted to free herself from this pattern. We performed a ritual in which she blessed and forgave Rick and asked for his forgiveness for any ways in which she might have hurt him in the past. She sent him on his way with unconditional love. She declared for herself her wholeness and her intent to attract the love that was right for her.

Linda and Rick had shared a strong karmic relationship, but one that had never grown into soulmate love. Unconditional love is the glue that binds all things in creation together. Unconditional love is what brings us back to the Source of All Being. A soulmate relationship deepens our understanding and expression of love. It deepens our self-understanding and helps us on our path to flower into our highest and best potential. But a soulmate relationship is not problem free.

Friends and Family Soulmates

We share different life experiences with souls who are close to us. We can recognize soulmates in our family and circle of friends. Perhaps we have the feeling that we have been friends or family before in other roles. Our bonds with these soulmates are, like our romantic soulmates, deep, harmonious, and long lasting. We may share a telepathic and empathetic rapport that creates an unspoken and complete understanding of one another. Being separated causes sorrow and longing.

The One Soulmate

Our ultimate soulmate is God. Our great mystical traditions teach that the spiritual task and evolution of the human soul is to reunite with the Creator. Throughout the ages, the human heart has looked for ways to be close to God through love, prayer, meditation, devotion, service, purification, and practice of virtues.

Our mystical relationship with God takes the form of a sacred marriage. We and God are the Beloved. The literature of the Christian saints tells of the mystical marriage, an ecstatic experience in which the soul is united in a special bond with God. Saint John of the Cross said spiritual marriage "is a total transformation in the Beloved in which each surrenders the entire possession of self to the other with a certain consummation of the union of love. . . . I think that this state never occurs without the soul's being confirmed in grace. . . . It is accordingly the highest state attainable in this life."

The visionary experience may include an actual wedding ceremony, in which a mystical ring is given to the saint. The ring may not be visible to others. For example, Saint Catherine dei Ricci experienced a mystical espousal to Christ in 1542. In her visionary experience, Christ placed a diamond and gold ring on the forefinger of her left hand "as a pledge and proof that thou dost now, and ever shalt, belong to Me." Others occasionally glimpsed the ring but usually saw just a raised and red ring of flesh around the finger.

Records exist of nearly 100 saints experiencing mystical marriage, with 55 of them receiving a mystical ring.

The marriage with God is often expressed in the same sensual, even erotic, language we use for human love. "I have no longer either soul or heart; but my soul and heart are those of my Beloved," said Saint Catherine of Genoa.

"The closer I am to the embrace of God, the sweeter is the kiss of God," said Saint Mechtilde of Magdeburg. "The more lovingly we both embrace, the more difficult it is for me to depart. The more God gives me, the more I can give and still have more. The more quickly I leave the Lord, the sooner I must return. The more the fire burns, the more my own light increases. The more I am consumed by love, the brighter I shall shine! The greater my praise of God, greater my desire is to love the Lord."

Our earthly soulmate relationships are part of our return to oneness with God. They open us to the profound depths of love and light a pathway for the soul.

4
Enchanted Meetings and Unions

Whoever loved, that loved not at first sight?

—CHRISTOPHER MARLOWE

Soulmate relationships truly are different from other relationships. They have distinguishing characteristics. In talking with many people about their soulmate experiences, I heard the same things over and over again. Certainly, every partnership is unique. But soulmate relationships have a profile that can be distilled into six common traits. These traits are shared by many, but not necessarily all, soulmate relationships.

1. You feel you were guided to meet.

Many people pray, meditate, visualize, affirm, and do rituals for finding their soulmate. Through these actions, intention is set, which organizes forces in the universe. I certainly asked to find my soulmate in that mystical moment on the beach, as well as in prayer and meditation that followed. Sometimes we organize universal forces simply by holding the hope that we will meet the right person during a trip or at an event.

We may be guided to meet our soulmate by our intuition or what feels like a spiritual power directing us. Perhaps we get a strong urge to go someplace or do something without knowing why, but we follow through on the feeling—and meet our soulmate.

Ken followed inner instructions to find a new home and then to go, of all places, to the laundromat.

I was directed to my soulmate. I had been out of a very bad marriage for about a year and had been renting a room from some friends. I decided it was time to find a place of my own. The first place I found seemed quite comfortable and reasonably priced, but I felt I should look around some more. I went to several other places, some in better condition than the first; however, they did not feel right. I was driving by the first place and got a strong feeling: *Something is supposed to happen here.* I went immediately and signed the papers to move in.

I had lived there for over a month and had not really thought any more about feeling directed to move there. Then one day as I was going about my daily routine, I received a strong message: *You need to go to the laundromat. You are going to meet a woman there.* This was in the form of a thought, but it was not prefaced with *I* but with *You.* It was much more forceful than a normal thought and in no way seemed to be my own.

I started gathering up my dirty clothes at my normal pace, slow. Again, another message came with the same qualities and force as the first message: *You need to hurry, or she will be leaving when you get there.* I quickly gathered my things and hurried to the laundromat.

As I was walking up, there was a beautiful young woman going in ahead of me. This laundromat was about three miles from the complex I lived at. Sarah and I struck up a conversation easily and comfortably. We soon found out in the course of the conversation that she lived one door down from me, but we had never seen each other. We started seeing each other regularly and shared a romantic relationship for about a year. We are still best of friends, see each other regularly, and love each other very much.

Nancy L. met her soulmate because her intuition told her which new home to buy.

When I separated from my husband, I was very frightened and lonely. I was looking for a townhouse to buy and had looked at forty-five to fifty homes. I narrowed it down to five and solicited my sister and brother-in-law to help me make my final decision. We arrived at the house that I eventually chose just after a heavy rainstorm, and as we pulled up out front a huge rainbow appeared in the sky and pointed down directly at the house. We all stared at it in wonderment and appreciation, and I also noticed that the house next door had a beautiful cat in the upstairs window looking down at us. I love rainbows and cats, and the most peaceful feeling I have ever had washed over me, and told me that *this* was the house that I had to buy. I loved everything about it, and started the process.

I ended up buying the house from a divorced lady who told me about a "single again" group. I joined the group the following week. It turned out to be a godsend because it helped me immensely, and I made many new friends who understood the process of divorce and separation.

The first week I was in the group, we all went out for a birthday celebration, and there was a good-looking guy who attended that I was immediately attracted to because of his wit and gentleness. He was a friend who worked with the woman from whom I had bought the townhouse, and she told me she had been trying to get him to join our group. He didn't join at that time (June), but showed up at the end of October. We bonded immediately, and in December we started dating.

Well, he turned out to be my soulmate beyond a shadow of a doubt. We have so much in common it's uncanny, and he makes me happier than I've ever been in my whole life. I truly believe an angel was watching over me the day that I saw the rainbow and the cat, and it led me to my new house, my new life, my new friends, and the love of my life.

Soulmates and rainbows seem to go hand in hand. Nancy's story reminded me of the rainbows that graced my own wedding. There are more rainbows to come in the stories of others.

Sometimes the hand of God works quietly in the background to bring two lovers together. The meeting between barbershop singers Sandy and Harry seemed unexpected and not obviously significant, but it soon revealed itself to both of them as a definite part of God's plan.

Nine years ago my soulmate and I happily and unexpectedly bumped into each other, that is to say, our paths finally crossed. I had seen Harry a few years before that afternoon singing his heart out at a barbershop function. I belonged to the female counterpart of that style of singing. I didn't notice any bells and whistles then, but somehow I know my own soul made a mental note to make us wait until our lives were in order for our meeting—our time to get reacquainted in this lifetime.

Our previous lives [note: not past lives, but previous paths in this life] found Harry living in a neighboring prairie province and I on an island in our Pacific Northwest. God, however, was already at work arranging our lives from behind the scenes, and we unknowingly went along for the ride.

The first big hurdle to our meeting was removed twenty-one years ago when we both moved to the same city in my province of British Columbia. Of course, we knew nothing of each other. Nevertheless, God did, and I guess He checked off one part of the equation as having been solved.

Only a few years after my move to Victoria, I found myself on my own. I was feeling none other than relief and happiness, as I knew my life in my new city still held some surprises. I had made some mistakes, or so they appeared, but I now believe there are no mistakes, only blessings given to us as lessons to learn in this earthly life.

I remember the day I got out of that mistake manifesting itself as an unsuccessful marriage. I moved into a peaceful place and, looking into my backyard for the first time, saw that there sat a boat. The boat triggered a memory from happy days gone by, but the name on the boat was a message spelled out for me. In large letters it read FREEDOM. It was like a sign from God I was on the right track.

Music was the medium that God used to bring Harry and me together. Thank you, God! That day, we met due to our love of music—as far as we knew. I had asked Harry's quartet to sing for our lady's chorus. His eyes met mine, and he answered, "I'd be honored!" For a moment, our eyes locked, and my soul knew those words pertained to much more than the subject of singing.

Less than a year later, we shared a love like neither one of us had ever known. We also committed to sharing the same address! Harry had come out of a marriage where the word *compatible* didn't exist, and for a while he was a little frightened of all we had in common. It was something he had never experienced, but before long he was able to relax, realizing this was real and all part of God's plan and His creation.

We soon found a church we both felt very comfortable being members of, and also formed a gospel trio to entertain our new church family. Surely it was another part of God's plan for us! Life was good! Soon Harry could be heard chanting around our home, "I love my life, I love my life!"

2. Your initial meeting is charged with compelling energy.

The room or space around you may suddenly change shape, and you may feel disoriented. The other person may seem lit with or surrounded by an unusual aura of light. Interestingly, there is a physical correlation to this phenomenon. Brain research with MRI (magnetic resonance imaging) at University College London shows that certain areas of the brain literally light up with increased blood flow when we see someone we love.

Sophie described:

I had a strange and beautiful feeling. We were attracted to each other like iron and magnet. There was light and warmth about him, like a golden light coming from his heart to meet and surround me, and this light was making me breathless and happy. It was a very pure and intense feeling of love.

An electrical shock may pass between you. When Yvette and Peter Bigger first touched hands, a shock passed through both of them. Tawanna and Mark felt as though a giant, invisible magnet was pulling them together.

There may be a locking of eyes that reveals the depths of souls and the knowledge that the two of you are meant to be together. Intuition expert and author Marcia Emery had been single for thirteen years, during which she had rarely connected with anyone "remotely interesting," as she put it. Prior to traveling out of state to give a workshop at a conference, Marcia said she "nourished the hope" that she would meet someone interesting there. She did—her future husband.

When I went to the registration table to get my room key and other materials, I was told, "A man has been asking for you. He's the Yoga instructor."

I replied in surprise, "The Yoga instructor! Where is he?"

They said he was in the next room. As I entered the room, I saw a handsome, tan-faced man standing near the fireplace. I walked across the room toward him and suddenly our eyes met. I didn't fall over, but it sure felt like the room went into a lopsided tilt during the three-minute interval when not a word was spoken.

When Diane and John met in a seemingly chance way, they both experienced a mysterious flash of light from the eyes. Diane was driving a girlfriend home, and along the way they passed a man driving in his truck. They didn't know him but waved, and he followed them down the road to where they stopped outside the girlfriend's apartment.

> I jumped out of my car to say hi to him, when to my utter amazement, when he opened the door of his truck to say hello, a light flashed from his eyes to mine. I didn't acknowledge what I saw, and neither did he, until later. I gave him my phone number, and an hour later, he called. We were surprised to find out how similar we were and that we both wanted kids and marriage. I then asked if he had seen something when we'd met, but before I could finish my sentence he said, "That flash of light," and I started getting so excited and said, "Yes, yes." He saw it, too. I'm convinced and most assured I have met my soulmate and am now married to him.

For musicians Sandi and Jeff, the eyes also were the heart and soul connection.

> Jeff and I met when we were both in our late thirties. I had been divorced for three years and decided not to date anymore. I was tired of starting new relationships that didn't last. Jeff had never been married and had given up hope of meeting the right person. Neither of us was looking for someone to date.
>
> Then one night we both were hired to play in the same community orchestra near the town where we both lived. During the first rehearsal, I felt the principal bass player (Jeff) staring at me, the principal flute player. Whenever I looked in his direction, he was looking at me. There was a strong connection in those first gazes that seemed deeper than just physical attractiveness.
>
> After the concert, Jeff asked for my phone number, and we had

our first date shortly thereafter. We immediately connected at our first dinner when he mentioned the name of Joseph Campbell, whose work is of great interest to me. We dated daily for two years before we were married.

Today we are more in love than ever. We consider ourselves extremely lucky to share such a passion for each other, for life, for music, for art, for our dogs, for our church, and for my children.

In some cases, the charge of energy does not take place in the initial meeting but at the point of recognition that the two of you are soulmates. "Paul and I recognized each other as soulmates when he first kissed me," said talk show host Laura Lee of her husband, Paul Robear. "I literally heard bells and saw stars and felt this energetic pulse run through us. A key was turned in the lock, and I stepped through the door. I felt transformed."

The kiss came on their first date. Prior to that, Laura Lee and Paul had known each other through mutual friends. They were attracted to each other but didn't act on it because they were involved with other partners.

One day Paul gave Laura Lee a ride. A strange thought entered her mind: *Oh, this is the man you're going to marry.* At the same time, Paul had an odd thought: *This is the girl you're going to marry.* Both of them dismissed the thoughts; neither was in a hurry to get married.

But after the first date, an evening out to dinner, life changed dramatically for both of them. Said Laura Lee:

After the first date, nobody else looked interesting. We moved in together immediately and went into that hibernation that new couples do. He proposed to me a week after we met. We waited a year—we wanted to go through all four seasons with each other first. I kept thinking, *I'm really enjoying my single life. I want this to happen, but not now.* But everything and everyone else just fell away. Our minds and hearts were focused on each other. We couldn't *not* get married—we were compelled.

Intuition expert and author Nancy Rosanoff met her husband, John Krysko, at a spiritual lecture in New York City. They struck up a conversation. John was looking for an assistant to help him; Nancy (not yet an author) was in need of a job. Everything seemed professional at first. John was dating several women; Nancy was separating from her husband. There was, however, an undercurrent of attraction that would not go away.

One day they were out for coffee to discuss business. "We were sitting there at the table, and we fell in love," said Nancy. "It just came over us. We both got it at the same time. We sat there looking at each other, both recognizing what had happened." They took a walk through Central Park. "We kissed in the park," Nancy said. "It was an incredible kiss."

3. You immediately or quickly feel like you know each other well, and that this person is the one meant for you.

Upon meeting your soulmate, you are unsettled and possibly shocked by the certainty that this is the one, or at least that a relationship of great importance is about to happen. Perhaps you know you are going to marry that person, even though you know nothing about them.

Carol received such a jolt when she passed by the table of a strange man in a restaurant.

We met by chance in a restaurant. I was with an acquaintance, and he was alone, sitting and eating at the bar. He kept turning around and looking at me. At the time, I believed he was irritated because we were laughing. Anyway, I did notice him turning around. When I went to the rest room and passed by, I commented to him "what a nice aquarium" was there in the restaurant, and he said, "Oh yes."

It was dark, and I could not really see him very well. But at that moment I said to myself, *Oh my God, I am going to marry this man!* When we met, *instantly* it was as if we were reunited and had always known each other.

He is from Japan and I was born here in Los Angeles. I am not Japanese. He is somewhat psychic and has always told me he knew we would be together, even when he was age thirteen in Japan. He says that is why he came to the United States. It is such a miracle we met, and I cannot imagine what it would be like if we did not meet—I really do think we might both not be here. He always knows where I am; we are very close.

John Krysko knew immediately that Nancy Rosanoff was the one, and he felt they were destined to be together. He called the other women he was dating and said, "I know this sounds strange and it's out of the blue, but I've met the woman I'm going to marry, and I can't see you anymore."

Nancy, still caught in the tangle of an ending marriage, was less certain at first. After two years, they married. "I like to think of soulmates as a conscious choice we make," said Nancy. "I consider John my divine lover and life mate, someone I chose to be with."

Said John, "Some part of Nancy's essence and my essence will always be linked, no matter what."

The sense of deep familiarity creates an aura around soul-mates that other people sense. At the conference where Marcia Emery and Jim met, an observer watching them talk together commented to a friend of Marcia's that they were going to get married.

Similar reactions from friends and others were experienced by Laura Lee and Paul Robear. "Other people could see some-thing between us, that we looked like we belonged together," said Laura Lee.

Lucy, who had just met her soulmate, found that others came up to them to comment on how happy they looked together. One man, she said, "said that someday he wished he could ex-perience the kind of relationship we had. When we revealed how we had just met, he replied, 'This is incredible. Everything happens for a reason. You two are soulmates. I want to be invited to the wedding!' "

4. As the relationship develops, you enjoy great harmony and happiness together.

Soulmates have their arguments just like everyone else, but their relationships with their partners overall are smooth and happy. Magazines and talk shows are filled with people who say that a successful marriage is hard and requires a lot of work. But to soulmates, their harmony often feels effortless, as though it is the most natural thing in the world to be completely at ease in a relationship.

"A soulmate is a person who you connect with on a deep level about how you both perceive life," said Paul Robear. "It's someone whose way of viewing life is not necessarily the same as yours but complements yours, so that there is not a compromise, there is a complement."

Laura Lee said:

We're very different in our personalities, but we're very much the same in our tastes, desires, and goals, and we have perfectly matched talents. We know what each other is thinking. We find each other's presence is like a sanctuary—we totally trust one another. Our spiritual work and our romance are intertwined.

When we would sit quietly in meditation, we would feel this energy envelop both of us, as though the air would have a certain quality. We still get that. Once in a past-life workshop, the facilitator saw an aura around us like a figure eight.

Soulmates are so good to each other, so good for each other, that being around them is like a fountain of youth. You feel like you're in a groove, everything is working for you, and the sun is shining on you, just from being in each other's presence. Other relationships can wear you down, even pummel you.

Said spiritual teacher Yvette Bigger:

We have complete trust. With other relationships, you have to build trust up. With Peter it was already there, from the very beginning. We understand each other's needs without saying anything. We already know what we have to give. We don't have to work at it, but we don't take it for granted, either. We're open about everything. We don't have any secrets—we don't have any need for secrets. Everything is unspoken, but we do say it, because that's important.

I don't need Peter and he doesn't need me, but we love to be in each other's company and to share things. We're free in each other's company. A lot of people don't feel free in their marriage.

Ken, who met his soulmate at the laundromat, said, "While I am quite comfortable being by myself, when I am with Sarah, my spirit soars. Doing the most mundane tasks in her company can become a great pleasure."

Said Sandi about Jeff:

My husband and I are perfect complements of each other, or as he says, "You are the other half of my puzzle." We love being together—at home, traveling, anywhere. Even when we are not physically together there is a warm, calm assurance that the spirit of the other is always present. I believe that our relationship will last beyond death—nothing can separate our bond.

Carol said:

The first two years together we were totally obsessed with each other (probably still are), but during those first two years, we could hardly even work. At the same time, we both went through about four years of healing from life experiences. This is hard to explain, but we know we were together before and for some reason were separated during this lifetime. I went through a sort of anger period, thinking why were we apart? Life would have been so much different for both of us had we always been together. We are still never apart and if so, talk on the phone several times a day. After we met I said, I now know life was worthwhile. Even if we had only had one day together, I would now consider my life worthwhile. We consider our time together a gift. We really do not like to share our time, even now, with anyone else. He has a beautiful spirit, very poetic, and loves all nature.

I have many friends who are married and none are like us. I have learned not to share with others about this relationship, as it has caused a few of my friends to cry or get upset. Mostly that would happen when I started talking about our relationship. Both of our worlds revolve around each other. We are the center of each other's world. We were both married before in marriages where we did not and maybe could not love the person.

You ask the quality of a soulmate? I think if someone has to ask, they do not have one. When you meet one, there is no question whatsoever. It is a meltdown that can last for several years— but in reality you have to go to work and live your life. Here is the bottom line: If we never had to be separated, we would not be, at all. We are the most happy and complete only when in each other's presence.

Soulmate qualities are: You come first with each other. You really do not like to be apart from each other. Your life feels complete and fulfilled once you are together. You are motivated to achieve your highest accomplishments (I built a very nice business over the past four years). You feel happy and contented on every level. The compatibility with your soulmate is on every level, emotional, physical, and intellectually.

An example of our normal day is, he does not want to leave for work in the morning. One to two hours later we talk for a short time on the phone and again maybe two more times before he comes home (just short calls to say "I love you" and "Be careful"). Many times he comes home early and calls laughing, "I am on the way home!"

We are very respectful of each other. I will always thank him for something he does for me; I do not take him for granted. This whole world can think anything they want of us, but we take care of each other.

Sandy C. observed:

Soulmates is that feeling of coming home as opposed to going home, as our minister talked about one Sunday. Coming home is that warm family-like feeling, all warm fuzzied, with none of the apprehension that going home sometimes carries due to past troubles and problems. It's hard to believe we ever had other lives before we met. It's like the lessons we are to learn in this lifetime have been made easier because we are together.

For Sophie, her soulmate relationship involves a merging of two into one.

I have the distinct feeling that we are advancing toward a completion, a peak, an experience of total and absolute love. And that we'll experience it together and be only one soul. I have visions of gold, light, transparent skies, paradise. We're already united in Heaven. In a way this love is already a success. It just has to be borne out of the Spirit into the earthly world.

5. The relationship stays fresh.

Soulmates use the same words to describe the vitality of their relationships: "still like teenagers," "fascinated," "giddy feeling," and "like being in love for the first time."

Brian Clarke, a friend of Paul and Linda McCartney, said that throughout their marriage they were "like teenage lovers, holding hands, giggling. They were fascinated with one another."

Others echo these feelings. "Paul [Robear] and I got married in 1988, and we still feel like newlyweds," said Laura Lee. "We never get tired of each other. He's continually fascinating to me."

Soulmate unions have a natural resistance to some of the hazards that are deadly to many long-term relationships. Soulmate unions are not likely to become boring, predictable, or stale. They retain a freshness and excitement even many years into the relationship. The electricity that sparks when soulmates first meet doesn't diminish. Time seems to pass quickly. Seven years into my relationship with Tom, it seems to me that I only met him a few months ago. Marcia Emery noted that seventeen years later, their wedding still seemed recent, as though it had only happened a year earlier. Their relationship, she said, is "joyous."

Sandy C. said:

Life is easy, life is warm, compassionate, natural, and meant to be! We have everything in common, we are best friends, and our love just keeps getting deeper. We become more and more sure of the fact we are soulmates! Nine years together is coming up.

We have bought a cute little house—a house I had actually visualized—a little white house with green shutters, matching window boxes, and a white picket fence. For years this image has represented to me a symbol of marital bliss, warmth, and a home that makes angels smile! God and the angels know the sign on the door reads, "Soulmates Live Here!"

We are soulmates from lives already lived. We thank God every day for our constant blessings and for arranging yet another life spent as one. Harry wears a beautiful diamond wedding ring. The gold band bears an inscription describing our relationship as we see it. It states, "Our destiny—God's creation."

6. You have a sense of sharing other, past lives with the other person.

Soulmates often feel they have had significant relationships together in other, past lives. Such relationships were not necessarily romantic but may have been familial. Sometimes soulmates don't know precise details but have a "knowing" of previous times together.

"Paul and I have a sense of sharing past lives, especially as brother and sister," said Laura Lee. "I think we're cut from the same soul group cloth. We feel we're part of the same soul family. We were destined to be together and made some sort of agreement to find each other in this life."

Yvette and Peter Bigger also feel a past-life link. Said Yvette:

I felt I had known Peter before from the very first moment I saw him. I wasn't too sure how I knew—I just had a very strong sensation and was confused by it. By the time we started dating, I had to come to an understanding about how I knew him. I asked in prayer and meditation to be shown. I saw we had been brother and sister.

Soulmates may have spontaneous flashes of specific past lives. In the first moments of meeting Jim, Marcia Emery saw the two of them in a past life together.

As I gazed into Jim's eyes without exchanging a single word, I clearly saw a familiar American Indian warrior. I felt I had known and loved him in another lifetime. Jim later shared that when he first saw me, he flashed back to a past life when I was a tall African male and he was my adoring wife. This puzzling imagery was a stark contrast to the reality of my short height and Caucasian skin.

Ken said about Sarah:

I strongly feel we have known each other in previous lives. One day when I was conversing with her eight-year-old son, he got a big grin on his face and stated, "My mom and you used to dream about each other before I was born." When I said "What!" he repeated it again word for word. I have no doubt this is true and that if I lose her again in another life I will dream of her again. I share something with Sarah I have shared with no other. My love for her is as eternal as my spirit and will travel with me from this life into the next, as it has before.

The feeling of sharing past lives can take people by surprise, especially if they have no opinions about reincarnation or do not believe in it. More of the past-life connection is explored in the next chapter.

5

You Have Known Each Other Before

I was originally little Gwion,
And at length I am Taliesin.

—TALIESIN

I had strong and spontaneous memories of past lives during the early stages of my relationship with Tom. By "memories" I mean recollections, glimpses, and understandings of past lives. I have always believed in reincarnation and had a sense of living before in certain time periods—and even having certain occupations—but these were more intuitive feelings than actual memories. Even my experiences in past-life regressions were not as vivid as the dreams and visions that I experienced then.

These experiences stopped after a time, but I believe that they were quite purposeful. My coming together with Tom triggered them as part of the reunion. They helped me to remember who I am.

Many soulmates have similar experiences, regardless of their views on reincarnation. As we saw in the previous chapter, they meet and simply know they have shared other lives in other times. Perhaps they have visions or dreams as well.

Soulmates in Ancient Egypt

One of the most unusual soulmate reunions on record is the story of Dorothy Eady. Her story involves one of the most powerful and exotic figures of ancient Egypt, Sety I. Their passion for each other was illicit, and in their fall from grace they were separated for more than 3,000 years. Dorothy lived her past life so intensely that it is difficult to dismiss it as imagination.

In 1907, three-year-old Dorothy tumbled down a flight of stairs in her London home and was pronounced dead by a doctor. An hour later, the child was revived completely and seemed to suffer no injuries or ill effects from her terrible fall. But the shock and trauma of the accident jarred something loose in her soul memory.

Dorothy soon began having strange dreams of a large building with columns and an exotic garden. She cried that she was not "home," but didn't know where "home" was. On a visit to the British Museum, the child was excited by Egyptian artifacts and declared she had found her people. By age seven, she identified the building in her dreams as the temple of Sety I, pharaoh of Egypt in the Nineteenth Dynasty, who lived from 1306 to 1290 B.C. As she grew older, she pursued an intense study of Egyptian history. Her story is chronicled in the book *The Search for Omm Sety: A Story of Eternal Love* by Jonathan Cott.

In 1918, she awoke one night to see a face bending over her—the face of the mummy of Sety. The hands and arms of the figure moved, but it said nothing. Dorothy found herself overcome with shock, astonishment, and above all, joy. The figure of Sety tore open her nightgown, and she shrieked. Her mother awakened and hurried to her room. Dorothy explained it away as a nightmare but could not explain how her nightgown had gotten torn open.

Secretly, Dorothy hoped she would meet Sety again. She began having a recurring dream in which she was a young Egyptian girl who was beaten with a stick for refusing to answer questions. The man who beat her was dressed like an Egyptian high priest.

Gradually, a truth was revealed to her: She and the pharaoh Sety, who was in his early fifties, had been passionate lovers. She had been a fourteen-year-old orphan, Bentreshyt ("Harp-of-Joy"), who served as priestess of Isis in Sety's temple at Abydos, the building she had seen so often in her dreams. At age twelve, she took vows to remain a virgin and be temple property. She fell in love with Sety, however, and became pregnant by him. The temple high priest tried to beat the truth out of her, but rather than reveal it, she took her own life.

At age fourteen in her present life, Dorothy knew that her heart and soul belonged to Sety. There could be no other love.

As she grew older and began to meet and date young men, Dorothy searched for one who would be most like Sety. She favored Egyptian men, but none could come close to her dream lover. She turned down several proposals of marriage.

Dorothy intuitively knew that in order to truly reunite with Sety, she would have to move to Egypt. At the age of twenty-nine, she consented to marry an Egyptian man and went to live in Cairo. Egypt itself served as a portal through time, enabling Dorothy to resume her 3,000-year-old love affair with the spirit of Sety. She had visions and saw ghosts at many Egyptian ruins. At night in her sleep, she traveled out in her astral body and was visited by Sety. She worshiped the ancient Egyptian gods. She bore a son, whom she named Sety. But after three years, her husband grew weary of her obsession with ancient Egypt, and he divorced her.

She took a job with the Egyptian Department of Antiquities in Cairo, which gave her access to research materials and to the antiquities themselves. She became known as Omm Sety and was regarded as an eccentric Englishwoman. At night, she was often seen praying in front of the Sphinx, making "queer gestures" and mumbling strange words in an unknown language. She was performing worship to Horus, for Sety had told her that the Sphinx was a representation of that falcon-headed Egyptian god, the son of Isis and Osiris.

Dorothy's divorce freed her to renew a sexual relationship with Sety. One night as she slept and dreamed, he sent the spirit of an ancient Egyptian priest to fetch her in her astral body. She awoke and grew very light, and followed the priest through a black fog until they arrived at Sety's palace at Amenti, the Egyptian underworld that is the land of the dead. Inside was Sety, who proposed that from then on, he would materialize to her in solid form as he had appeared when they were lovers, as a vigorous man in his early fifties. She consented, and he did so, appearing often and making tender and passionate love to her. He told her he intended to marry her at Amenti, but it could not happen until she left her life as Dorothy.

Dorothy desired to return to the temple of Abydos, even though it meant she would once again become temple property. The opportunity to do so presented itself in 1956. When she informed Sety, he told her that he would continue to visit her, but they would nevermore make love. If they resisted temptation during the rest of her life at the temple, their original crime would be forgiven, and they could be together for eternity.

Dorothy described in detail her last night of passion with the king: "That was the last night we ever made love together, and it was the sweetest. He has slept beside me many times since then, and we have embraced and kissed, but nothing more, because the Temple lies between us like a drawn sword." Sety told her, "If there is no temptation there is no test, but O Beloved, help me to be strong, and do not weep, I will never leave you or cease to love you."

In the village of Arabet Abydos, Dorothy worked at a low-paying job as a draftswoman and helped in the restoration of her beloved temple. The strange Western woman who seemed so at home in the antiquities of Egypt mystified the locals, who feared her as a witch or adept of Egyptian magic. Living conditions were primitive—she lived in a mud-brick hut with no running water, plumbing, or electricity—but she was infinitely happy. Sety visited her often, and they spent nights in each other's arms but refrained from making love.

Once she asked him how it was he had known she had been born again on earth, and where to find her. He said that after long ages of suffering, Osiris had mercy upon him, and he was summoned before "the Council." The Council, who manifested only as disembodied voices in a great hall of black stone, seemed to be responsible for keeping the order in Amenti. Its members answered to Osiris. The Council informed Sety that Dorothy had been reborn, and he was permitted to search for her. He wandered as a spirit all over the world, until at last he'd found her. At first, he had been permitted only to appear in the form he last had on earth, that of a mummy. Later he was permitted to appear as a spirit and then as a living man. He had chosen his early fifties as his form, for that was when he had been happiest.

Dorothy rarely spoke of her secret life to anyone, even close friends. She kept her confidences in her diaries.

Dorothy died on April 21, 1981. She was buried facing west, toward the Land of the Dead, in the desert north of the Sety and Ramses temples. Undoubtedly her freed soul headed straight for the palace at Amenti, for the long-awaited reunion with Sety, her soulmate and lover for all eternity.

Roman Lovers

Helene's soulmate union with her husband, Victor, led to a past-life recall that provided Helene with many insights into the present.

When I was in my midthirties and my husband, Victor, was going through health challenges, I was intuitively directed to have a past-life regression. I was searching for some kind of deeper understanding of us. Victor has done a lot of spiritual growing through health challenges, a difficult situation for me.

I found myself in Greece. I was being trained as a priestess in the healing arts. I was in a beautiful environment and surrounded by feminine support of the deepest nature. I saw myself standing on the shore and seeing a boat leave. I knew it was Victor then and that my heart longed to follow him. The scene then changed. I had followed him to Rome or a town on the outskirts of Rome. He was a Roman governor and married to a Roman woman. He set me up as a mistress in this small house. I had left my training and my home ground. I was deeply unhappy. I was living in a city environment, and the stimuli were bombarding my senses severely as I picked up every vibration surrounding my little place. I was secondary to his primary life, as he could not integrate me because of his status. He visited often, but as time progressed, I got more and more depressed. Then I became pregnant. I saw myself aborting through the use of herbs and dying in his arms. He was beside himself in sorrow.

This past regression put so many things in place for me:

—How the moment he met me he recognized my essential gold and told me about it. How he immediately wanted to marry me. I was not ready. After we eventually married, I kept my maiden name. He would always tell people when we gave our names that even though we had different names, we were married. Until then I had never understood why he did that.

—How he wrote a story about us, shortly after we met, about how we would get married, how we would live at the ocean and have a little girl called Elizabeth. We did marry, we did live at the ocean (so important to my well-being), and at one point thought of having that little girl. Somehow both of us knew that it would be a little girl. Then he got very ill (it was around the time I had the past-life regression), and my dreams told me that unless things changed, he would die. I remember then deciding that I would not have a child, that I did not want to be left alone with a child. He worked his way through this situation, and after that, we decided not to have a child. I think he was also concerned because of his epilepsy.

A year ago on a vacation to Sedona, Elizabeth showed up in a vision next to me in a train journey, now a young woman. I guess at some level of reality we did have that child. She looked a lot like me and I felt deep love for her. I cried that day a lot when I got to the hotel because we had not had her in this physical reality.

In this lifetime from the beginning of our relationship he always put me first. I used to get upset about that. In the Roman days he was about the same height he is now but more muscular and definitely more macho, so to speak. He had put me second to all.

Then he also was the picture of health and power. He had achieved a lot in the sensory world in terms of power, money, and recognition. In this lifetime he dealt with illness on and off and even though he is incredibly talented, having had careers in business, been a musician, a salesman, a motivational speaker, and had a couple of businesses of his own, misfortune seems to plague him in terms of achieving success. He supported my journey fully, and I was the one that succeeded in the sensory world. I became a managing director at a financial institution, having started as a file clerk when I arrived there. He supported me every inch along the way.

He also deeply honored my spirituality and ways of being. I am auditorily very sensitive and cannot listen too long to radio or TV. I am very sensitive to the feelings of voices. He has learned how to watch sports with the sound off and bought equipment so he can hear it without bothering me. I am very sensitive in a lot of ways, the difficult part of my gifts, and he has never complained and supported my sensitivities completely. It all seemed to come second nature to him.

He also has such a strange mix of health and illness. When well, he exudes incredible health like he has never been sick one day in his life. During those times he reminds me of that Roman governor. This lifetime he has chosen illness as a teacher of spirit. He had a recovery of a secondary illness a couple of years ago by doing sound meditation and now is in the grips of that same one, only deeper, doing the work to release it. He is in this lifetime like in that other one deeply interested in the workings of the sensory world, every little bit of it. But different from that time he has begun a journey of rediscovery at forty-two, a year before he met me, and then we met and we have been on this spiritual path together.

It was such perfect timing. The moment I met him I felt my life align in its purpose. Like he brought the memory of that with him in some intangible way. All the training I did not complete that lifetime I did in this one. And I also grounded in the sensory world, which was very important because I was so ungrounded and living so much in the invisible reality, preferring it over the visible one.

Family Ties and Best Friends

Many soulmates recall past lives together as family members, especially as brother and sister, as noted. The soul desires to have many experiences, and thus soulmates share different kinds of relationships as part of their soul growth.

Some who are romantic soulmates in the present feel they have been close, soulmate friends in previous lives. Dana said:

When I met my husband, I had the sense that I already knew him from before, even though we were strangers. As our relationship developed, this sense grew stronger. I think we were very good friends in a past life, and that we helped each other out in some way. Now we have come together to be lovers in the deepest sense of the word.

Platonic soulmates also may sense past-life connections. Said Eileen:

Brenda and I have been best friends since we were little. I met her when my family moved into a new house, and she was living in the one next door. Right from the start, I felt she was my best friend. As we have grown up, I have felt incredibly close to her. We always know what the other is thinking. Both of us have husbands, but we call each other soulmate. I have always had the feeling that we were close friends in at least one past life.

You may intuit a past-life link with your soulmate, even if you don't necessarily believe in reincarnation. If so, don't deny the thoughts. If you cannot accept reincarnation, think of the link as part of the continuity of life. The soul is eternal, and we are meant to learn its full dimensions and understanding.

6
Questions and Answers

For love is repaid with love alone.

—Saint Francis de Sales

In the preceding chapters, we've explored many of the characteristics of soulmate relationships. Here are additional questions that people ask:

Is it possible to miss or pass on your soulmate?

I hear from people who say they met someone whom they *knew* was their soulmate, but that person didn't recognize the same in them. They endured rejection, great frustration, and even anguish, feeling that the only love that was meant to be for them slipped through their fingers.

Sometimes these are cases of mistaken identity. We may be intensely attracted to someone and mistake the attraction for a soulmate connection. We may project soulmate onto someone who really doesn't fit the bill. Such projections usually arise out of fear and desperation; we fear being alone and we are desperate to avoid it. As you will see during the course of this book, we are best able to attract and connect with soulmates when we are in a positive, optimistic, and affirmative flow of energy.

Or, we've projected soulmate onto a lesser karmic balancing or unfinished business. Relationships that become abusive in any form are *not* soulmate connections.

Sometimes the timing isn't right. The other person may decide not to enter into an intense commitment. This may happen to both friendship soulmates as well as romantic soulmates, as in the following case of a woman who was married to her soulmate and then found a friendship soulmate.

I felt throughout my life that I also had a female soulmate somewhere out there. Six years ago, I met a woman with whom I instantly fell in love. It is the best way I can describe it. She was the first person I met who could speak and understand my deeper language. With my husband, our language was different, and we would communicate until we understood. With her, we just understood. I thought I had found my female soulmate.

Then one year ago, she began changing and rejecting me and our relationship. I have tried to work it out, but she has not been willing to talk about the change or even acknowledge what was going on. I ended the relationship because of the pain it inflicted on me to watch her lose interest in me. Today, I wrote a letter to her expressing how betrayed I felt. It took a long time for me to write this letter. During our five years together, there flowed between us the sweetest woman love and intimacy I experienced in my whole life. So I don't really understand why it is where it is. I thought for sure she was my female soulmate.

It is possible to miss or pass on soulmate connections. We all have free choice. If we are not sufficiently spiritually aware, we may miss the signals. We may choose to pass, for various reasons. Perhaps we have commitments to others. Perhaps we have not healed inner wounds that prevent us from participating in a soulmate relationship. Perhaps one soul partner grows more quickly than the other, and the two paths don't quite come together.

If such a situation of apparent missed connections has happened to you, do not despair. We have more than one chance to love in life. I believe that in any given lifetime, more than one soulmate will cross our path. The textures and tones of each relationship will be different, but they will all be part of the grand tapestry the soul weaves in its path to Oneness.

Can we all find the nurturing love we desire, one that will last? Yes we can, each and every one of us.

I'm married and have met my soulmate. What do I do?

In earlier times, people often married for advantage, class, and politics. You were fortunate if you developed a loving respect and regard for each other. You were doubly blessed if true love was part of the picture. Many examples from history attest to married couples finding their soulmate loves in extramarital affairs. Sometimes their spouses knew of these relationships and looked the other way. Divorce was seldom an option. If the marriage continued to function and provided other advantages and benefits, outside liaisons were tolerated. Men, of course, had far more liberties in this regard than women, who were expected to remain faithful to the marriage in all circumstances.

Many marriages around the world are still arranged today, sometimes when the prospective bride and groom are still small children. In the modern West, we have more freedom to choose our relationships. We expect fidelity.

Many people meet their soulmates after they have had experience in romantic relationships, including marriage. It is possible to meet your soulmate while you are married to someone else.

Ideally, however, one should be free of commitments prior to meeting a soulmate. If your marriage is not working, and you have done everything you can to make it work and still conclude that it is best to end it, then do not hang on to it like a safety net until you wait for something better to come along. It is best to be clear of other entanglements—personally, legally, karmically, and spiritually.

But for every ideal rule there are always exceptions. We need only look once again to history to see examples of famous relationships that were outside of marriage, or marriages that were broken in order to form new ones.

Vice Admiral Horatio Nelson was one of England's greatest naval commanders, a brilliant, magnetic man who was revered by his crews. He was adored by his loving spouse, Fanny, whom he married in 1787 as the perfect wife for an aspiring naval officer. Nelson was away at sea for all but five years of their married life, during which Fanny remained steadfast in her devotion to him. Nelson created an international scandal when he lost his heart and head to Lady Emma Hamilton, a young, vivacious former courtesan who was married to Sir William Hamilton, England's elderly ambassador to the court of Naples.

In 1798, fresh from a stunning victory over Napoleon's forces in the Battle of the Nile, Nelson put in at Naples for repairs. There Emma, whom he had briefly met five years before, gave him an emotional welcome, fussed over his minor wounds, and then turned him into a local celebrity. Placed on a pedestal before society and the royal court, Nelson was flattered by all the attention. He was dazzled with Emma, as she was with him, despite the fact that he'd lost his right arm and the sight of his right eye in previous battles.

In the thrall of infatuation and then love, Nelson stayed on at Naples for two years, openly conducting an affair with Emma while Sir William looked the other way. He neglected his naval duties, which angered his superiors in England, and hence was recalled to London in 1800. Arriving with Emma and Sir William, Nelson was hailed as a hero by the public. But high society snickered at his affair, and royalty snubbed him.

Nelson didn't care. He, Sir William, and Emma carried on a ménage à trois for three years while Fanny pleaded in vain for a reconciliation. After Sir William died in 1803, Emma and Nelson bought a luxurious house, where they lived with their daughter, Horatia, until Nelson was summoned back to duty two years later.

Joining battle with Napoleon's naval forces again, he demolished the French fleet in the Battle of Trafalgar, thereby establishing England as ruler of the seas. But the victory cost him his life. Nelson's last request as a dying man was that Emma be granted a pension from his estate, but the British government refused, awarding everything to Fanny and his brother. Emma died penniless, nine years later, in Calais.

A couple whose love changed the course of a nation were Wallis Simpson and King Edward VIII of England. For royalty, marriage usually is a matter of expediency, designed to cement political alliances, gain wealth, or ensure bloodline succession. But for Edward VIII, marriage was a matter of the heart, and he paid his lover, Wallis Simpson, the ultimate compliment by giving up the throne of England in order to marry her.

Wallis, an American raised in Baltimore, married her second husband, Ernest Simpson, an English businessman, in 1928. Their home in London was the scene of frequent, lively parties where diplomats, businessmen, aristocrats, and celebrities mixed in stimulating conversation. The Simpsons met Prince Edward in 1930 while staying in the countryside with friends. Soon the prince was attending dinners and parties at the Simpsons' home.

Although not a beauty, Wallis possessed a natural grace and dignity and was startlingly well informed about politics, current events, and the theater. She never hesitated to argue her views, and her spirited independence enchanted the prince. They shared a keen zest for living and spent an increasing amount of time together, dancing, partying, and traveling. Their friendship developed into love.

Edward ascended the throne on January 20, 1936. Eleven months later, he announced his intention to marry Wallis as soon as she was divorced from Ernest. His ministers balked; this was a serious matter of state. Not only did Wallis lack royal blood, but her divorce would not be recognized by the Church of England, of which Edward, as king, was head. It quickly became apparent that the only way for Edward to have Wallis without causing a major scandal and political crisis was to give up the throne.

Wallis, prepared to endure "rivers of woe, seas of despair and oceans of agony" for Edward, urged him to give her up. But Edward, unyielding in his love, abdicated on December 11, 1936, and the lovers immediately left England. As the Duke and Duchess of Windsor, they spent most of their remaining years together living in splendor in France.

Years later, the duchess stated, "Any woman who has been loved as I have been loved, and who, too, has loved, has experienced life in its fullness."

If you are married and think someone else is your soulmate, you must act responsibly. Marriage is a solemn commitment, not a convenience. Make certain you are not projecting your marital unhappiness onto someone, or that you have not idealized them.

It also may be important for you to wait to act for various reasons. Soulmates feel that they come together at the right time. Said LeAnn:

I found my soulmate six years before we came together. I was in a relationship at the time that still had to run its course. And my soulmate-to-be still had a lot of growing up to do. Always my guides told me that this person would be my future partner, and that timing was very important to us coming together. And it was. We came together at the right time in the right place and space for both of us. We connect very deeply and freely and give each other the space we need to grow. Not once in that six-year period did we have any sexual contact—we were nothing more than friends. When the time became closer, spirit brought us together, through accidental meetings and strange coincidences.

Do soulmates ever leave each other or divorce?

The ideal soulmate contract is for life. Some soulmate relationships do fulfill their purpose and come to an end of their own accord.

If you lose your soulmate in death, will you find another one?

Whenever we lose a loved one to death, especially a romantic partner, we wonder if we will ever be able to love again and if we will ever be loved. It's hard to imagine anyone ever stepping into the void that is left. As Paul McCartney said to the media of him and his family when Linda died, "We will never get over it, but I think we will come to accept it." He added that her death would leave a "huge hole" that would never be filled.

It's especially hard to lose a soulmate. Few people, however, would want the partners they leave behind to spend the rest of their days alone. The human soul is meant for companionship and relationships. What we learn from soulmate unions enables us to go forward and find love again. Nothing will ever replace the one who has gone, of course, but we have the ability to find another deep and meaningful relationship.

A year after Linda McCartney died, Paul told the media of his "unbearable" grief. Then he met model Heather Mills, and life and love were renewed. Those close to Paul felt that Linda would approve.

Poignant stories are recorded of soulmates who cannot bear to be separated by death, and choose, if possible, to die together. Isador Straus was the owner of the prestigious Macy's department store in New York City, and a philanthropist. He and his wife, Ida, were aboard the ill-fated *Titanic* that sank on its maiden voyage on April 15, 1912, after hitting an iceberg in the North Atlantic Ocean.

Throughout the forty-one years of their marriage, Isador and Ida were deeply devoted to one another. The length of their union never diminished the affection they displayed or their desire to be in each other's company. Whenever they had to be separated, they wrote to each other daily.

Ida resisted taking safety in a lifeboat as the *Titanic* went under. She gave her place to her maid. She went down with her beloved, clasped in a last embrace. Her decision not to leave Isador surprised none of their six children or their many friends, who well knew their mutual devotion. A memorial to them in a Bronx cemetery is inscribed, "Many waters cannot quench love, neither can the floods drown it."

The Strauses found themselves in dire circumstances that most of us will never have to face. Soulmate survivors will, like anyone, look for ways to carry on. Some may prefer to remain alone, at least for a long time. Others will want to share the joys of love again.

If you have been widowed, and the time is right to look for another relationship, set your intent on meeting someone else with whom you have a strong soul connection—possibly another soulmate!

Can astrology identify soulmates?

I've always appreciated what astrology can show us about the dynamics of life and relationships. I especially appreciate a comment attributed to astrologer Dane Rudhyar: "The stars impel, they do not compel." In other words, astrology can help us with our understanding of ourselves and others and to see opportunities and potential problems. But it does not mete out a destiny that cannot be changed.

Astrology is based on an ancient and universal concept that the physical world is a mirror of the heavenly world. "As above, so below," is one of the axioms of the Western mystery tradition. The position of the planets at the moment of your birth fixes your natal horoscope, which becomes the astrological blueprint of your life. Explanations for everything that happens to you throughout life are measured against this blueprint. The horoscope divides life into twelve houses, each governed by a sign of the zodiac.

Most people are familiar with their sun sign, the house occupied by the sun at the time they were born. Two other important signs are the moon sign, the house occupied by the moon at birth, and the ascendant, or rising sign, the sign of the zodiac that was rising on the horizon. The sun sign governs personality. The moon sign governs our emotional side. The rising sign governs the face we like to present to the world.

Astrology offers much more depth than these major signs, however. From their positions in the houses, the planets all make different kinds of angles with one another. Some angles are auspicious; others create negative tension. A person's natal chart never changes, but the charts for any particular day or time of life are fluid and reflect the changing positions of the planets.

We can get an astrological picture of a relationship through two types of charts. A synastry chart compares two charts. A composite chart is a unified chart: two charts merged together to reflect a partnership. According to astrology, both synastry and composite charts can reveal areas where two people will mesh harmoniously and where they will have difficulty.

Thus, astrology will not positively identify a soulmate for you. But it can provide important validation to what you are already feeling about a relationship. And it can help you gain more insight into the relationship.

When astrologers examine the horoscopes of two individuals for signs of compatibility, they look first for three significant factors: the relationships between the positions of their sun, moon, and rising signs. Conjunctions—the proximity of two planetary bodies, usually in the same sign—can signal harmonies that will help a relationship thrive through the years. Thus, if one partner's sun sign is Taurus and the other's moon sign is Taurus, that means their sun and moon are conjunct, or united. Other signs for happy relationships are conjunctions of both moons, and conjunction of the moon and ascendant. In fact, it has been an astrological tradition since the time of Ptolemy that one of these conjunctions—sun/moon, moon/moon, or moon/ascendant— is required for an enduring marriage. Unless there are astrological peculiarities, these conjunctions indicate a harmonious, complementary balance between the partners.

The great psychiatrist Carl G. Jung was interested in astrology and sometimes consulted the horoscopes of his patients in search of clues to their inner selves. He believed that astrology, like alchemy, originates in the collective unconscious, a layer of consciousness deep below waking thought which unites all human beings.

Jung's curiosity was aroused by the ancient traditional astrological and alchemical correspondences to marriage in terms of the three conjunctions. He undertook a study of the horoscopes of 483 married couples, randomly collected, to see how often these conjunctions appeared.

The results showed an unusually high number of all three conjunctions: sun/moon, moon/moon, and moon/ascendant. Jung examined the horoscopes in batches. The first batch of 180 marriages (360 horoscopes) revealed 10.9 percent with sun/moon conjunctions—a probability of 1 in 10,000. The second batch of 220 marriages (440 horoscopes) revealed 10.9 percent of moon/moon conjunctions—another probability of 1 in 10,000. The third batch of 83 marriages (166 horoscopes) revealed 9.6 percent moon/ascendant conjunctions, or a probability of 1 in 3,000.

What's more, the probability that all three conjunctions would show up in the horoscopes studied was 1 in 62,500,000. Marriage is such a complex relationship that one would not expect it to be characterized by any one or several astrological configurations, Jung said. He added that the improbability of the high incidence of these three conjunctions in the sample group being due to mere chance was so enormous that it necessitated taking into account the existence of some factor responsible for it. Jung said the horoscopes demonstrated synchronicity, or a "meaningful coincidence." Somehow, persons who were compatible according to their horoscopes had found each other and married. (However, Jung offered no comment upon the happiness or stability of the marriages in his astrological study. Nor did he think that the results of his study necessarily validated astrology.)

Other significant planetary relationships to consider for romance and harmony are between Venus and Mars. Venus represents love, appreciation of beauty, and the feminine; Mars represents action, sexual assertion, and the masculine. Two people who have significant angles—such as conjunctions—with their Venuses and Marses should experience an intense sexual and romantic attraction to each other, and find themselves compatible in many ways. These angles do not guarantee a soulmate connection nor longevity of the relationship, but I believe that enduring and deep relationships more often than not have these connections.

Shortly after I met Tom, he asked me what was my sun sign. I rolled an inner eye. *How seventies,* I thought. *Sixties, even!* Still, I told him. He asked for my birth date. I then thought he wanted to know how old I was. I said, "My birth date? Men should know better than to ask women their ages!"

"I don't care how old you are," he replied. "I want to do your chart."

Really seventies, I thought. I gave him the month and day but not the year. I refused. But I willingly told him where I was born. And yes, I knew my moon and rising signs, and gave them.

"Thanks," he said. I could tell by his smile that I'd given away the farm.

When Tom got home that night, he plugged the information into his astrology program and considered some possible years for my birth date. The first one he picked was it. Tom cast my natal chart and then a synastry chart between the two of us.

Once a skeptic about astrology, he had become genuinely interested in it when he saw how it corroborated qualities of relationships. He took some courses in astrology. He gathered up statistics and compared hundreds of relationships. Prior to meeting me, he had decided to check his own impressions against the stars. He was not using astrology to choose his dates but rather as a validation of his own intuition.

Our synastry chart showed a good sun/moon angle, though not the strongest one—a trine and not a conjunction. But we had four out of four possible Venus-Mars conjunctions, as well as numerous other compatible angles in various houses.

When I talked to Laura Lee and Paul Robear about their soulmate relationship, I learned that astrology had provided validation to them, too. Paul had consulted a Vedic astrologer. Vedic astrology, an Indian system, is different than the astrology used in the West. The reading was detailed and specific about the ideal person that would come into Paul's life. It turned out to be a precise match to Laura Lee. After they got together, Laura Lee had a reading, which matched Paul. The readings did not change their feelings but confirmed what they already felt.

If you are interested in astrology and are curious about what the stars have to say about your love life, consult a qualified astrologer. Consider the information as one of many perspectives. The stars show potential; it is up to us to take action and turn potential into reality.

7

Are You Ready for a Soulmate?

For love is heaven, and heaven is love.

—SIR WALTER SCOTT

Bringing new love into your life is an important undertaking. You must be very clear about what you want. You must be very honest with yourself in terms of changes you need to make in order to fulfill your dreams. Not only must you be available and open on the outside, you must be available and open on the inside. The inner preparation must come first, for it sets the stage for what will follow in the outer world.

Finding new love can seem daunting. We've all had our disappointments in love, and sometimes our hurts can make us less open to another relationship. Or we're afraid of failure, of trying and trying and not finding a new partner. If we had long-term relationships that came to an end, being single again seems alien.

Three Fundamental Truths

You will move to a new level in love by first accepting three truths:

Truth #1: "I am always loved."

It's easy to feel unloved when you're without a partner. Remember that love attracts love, and you will have a much easier time finding someone special when you are filled with love, surrounded by love, *and you know it*.

You are never without love. Perhaps you don't feel you are receiving it from the sources you desire, but other sources of love nourishment are ever-present. Everything in creation is bound together by the bond of unconditional love that flows from the Creator. We are born into life out of divine love. We are surrounded by the spiritual radiance of love from angels. This love is eternal and unchanging; it is always there, regardless of what happens to you in life.

You can connect with this love in simple ways. You can appreciate the beauty around you: the smell of flowers, the shape of trees, the affection of pets.

There are always people who love and appreciate you. Small kindnesses and generosities often generate the most love. Be considerate to others; their appreciation—even if given as a "thank you" or a nod of the head—is an expression of love.

The more you fill your life with an appreciation for nature, for what you have, and for the people in your life—even strangers you meet but once—the more you will build up an aura of loving energy within you. This radiates like a beacon. Who doesn't want to be around love? Make yourself a light of love, and others will be attracted to you.

Truth #2: "I am lovable and deserve to be loved."

You came into this life blessed by God as a worthy soul. All of us have flaws and shortcomings. Life is the process of working on those and improving ourselves. Within you is your core essence of worthiness. Never think that you are not worthy.

We lose our sense of self-worth when we are vulnerable to the criticisms and even abuse of others. The questions echo in our minds for years: "Why can't you do better?" "You're no good!" "You'll never amount to anything!" And sometimes worse.

A broken relationship can batter our sense of self-worth. We doubt our ability to love again or to attract a good partner. We play the old tapes from childhood or a previous relationship about our unworthiness.

But those tapes speak untruth. Erase those old tapes *now* and record a new one within: "I am lovable and deserve to be loved."

Truth #3: "I have the power to love."

Having the power to love is a significant step up from knowing that you are worthy and deserve to love. When you connect with your power to love, life can change in fast and dramatic ways. You *know* that you have the ability to bring love into your life.

Overcoming Obstacles to Your Goals

We like to set goals and dream dreams about reaching goals, finding love, and having a better life. But we often get in our own way when it comes to achieving those dreams. We have a lofty vision, a grand heart's desire—and then we get cold feet. Regardless of what it is we wish to attain—whether it's love or a new job or a career change altogether—we can be needlessly held back by one or more of the following fears:

"I don't know what to do."

I hear this one most frequently from people who are newly single after long-term marriages or committed relationships. The prospect of living as a single person, searching for a suitable partner, and reentering the dating world can be overwhelming.

Divorced at forty-three, Betsy was at a loss for what to do to meet men. Going to bars and singles parties were out. She knew all the conventional lore—attend concerts, go to meetings, get involved in activities—but she was afraid she would look transparent in motives to others. Years ago, she had done all those things. Now they seemed silly. So she stayed at home, convinced that it was preferable to awkward and perhaps futile dating experiences. For a while she was satisfied, but then she began to feel lonely. One night while in meditation and prayer, Betsy had the sudden insight that the men she would like to meet felt just as she did: uncertain and awkward about being single again. They would be glad to meet someone who made them feel at ease. By focusing on others instead of herself, and by doing visualization exercises, Betsy was able to venture out and explore opportunities for meeting men.

"I don't know what will happen if I do."

In other words, "I'm afraid of failing." Life, especially life lived to the fullest, requires risk-taking. We don't know the ultimate outcome of our efforts. Anytime we put ourselves on the line, we feel vulnerable. Sometimes we succeed, sometimes we don't. But nothing happens at all unless we try.

Laura N. created an obstacle for herself by spinning out fantasies of probable (and undesirable) outcomes. What if she got involved in a relationship and then had to make compromises in other areas of life? What if she had to play the role of stepmom? What if she had to move? What if she got dumped? What if, what if, what if!

I helped Laura to understand how our thoughts build up energy that attracts circumstances to us. Worry attracts exactly what you don't want. Anxiety creates negative visualizations that do the same. Laura learned how to release undesirable thoughts and worries and replace them with thoughts and images of what she did want. She also worked on establishing the presence of trust and faith in her life: trust that she would be guided to do the right things and faith that what she sought would come to pass.

A variation of this obstacle is the "if only" game: "If only I could be certain . . ." "If only I knew . . ."

Don't let uncertainty put a hold on your life.

"When . . . then . . ."

This is a delaying obstacle. The one heard most often from single women is, "When I lose ten pounds, then I'll go out and try to meet somebody." And how long does it take to lose the ten pounds? Maybe never!

"When-then" can take many forms: When you save money, you'll do something (take a trip, join a dating service); when you finish a phase at work, you'll have time for relationships; when you update your wardrobe, you'll feel like going out, and on and on.

Sometimes we have other things we say we need to do or finish before we allow ourselves to begin anew. It's certainly fine to take care of responsibilities and obligations, but do not substitute them for reasons not to pursue your goals.

Make an Assessment of Yourself

Before you can identify what you want in a soulmate, you have to know who you are and what you want in life. You have to know your own inner, deep truth. You must be completely candid about yourself with yourself. Otherwise, you may find yourself chasing illusions.

"You have to know your own flow," said intuition expert Nancy Rosanoff. A life has its own stream of energy in the river of all creation. When we go along with the flow, we gain an understanding of our own unique currents. We allow life to unfold in its most perfect order. We move in harmony with the greater cosmic flow toward harmony and wholeness.

Do a thorough assessment of yourself and what you want.

First, look at your previous significant relationship. Draw up a list of everything that you liked about it. What worked well? What made you happy? What made the two of you happy?

Next, draw up a list of what you did not like about the relationship and wished could have been different. What didn't work so well? What made you unhappy? What made your partner unhappy? Then, ask yourself what you are prepared to do differently in the next relationship.

Give yourself an honest appraisal. What do you have to offer a partner? What is appealing about you? What are your strong points? Why would someone be attracted to a committed relationship with you? Then, don't be afraid to look at what needs to change within you. For example, are you too dependent or independent? Are you still carrying around unfinished business from your previous relationship?

Your outer world is a reflection of your inner world. If you do not have your inner house in order, you will find yourself repeating the same patterns and mistakes in relationships.

Mistakes About Soulmates

Without knowing yourself, you may be vulnerable to mistaking a relationship for a soulmate. Here are the three most common mistakes to avoid:

Unrealistic expectations

Don't expect that the right relationship will make everything in life perfect and complete. While soulmates do enjoy a high degree of harmony, they nonetheless are two unique individuals, not carbon copies of each other.

"The most successful relationships enable people to be who they are," said Nancy Rosanoff. "A relationship has to be able to handle two very strong people. It's not two halves coming together to make a whole. It's two incomplete people coming together to create two complete people."

John, Nancy's husband, observed, "A soulmate is not the perfect other. A real soulmate will always provide a certain amount of tension that enables each person to grow and experience their deepest truth."

The sense of oneness experienced in a soulmate relationship is not the loss of individuality but a participation in union on a high level of being.

Fear of being alone

Another mistake people make is projecting "soulmate" onto someone in order to avoid being alone. Human beings are not meant to live in solitude, but in partnership and community. It is natural to not want to be alone. But the desire for partnership can create an unconscious fear of being alone and influence us to grab the first reasonable thing that comes along.

Many people meet their soulmate during a time when they are most comfortable as a single person. Take a cue from celebrities Barbra Streisand and James Brolin, both of whom had settled into lives without significant others before they met and fell in love. Streisand told the media that she was enjoying her solitude, while Brolin said he wasn't concerned with finding someone to make him complete.

Acceptance of turmoil

If a relationship is characterized by ongoing turbulence, distrust, or even abuse, it is *not* a soulmate relationship. Do not fool yourself into accepting that unhappiness and hardship between the two of you. All relationships go through ups and downs and must face external difficulties. But soulmates have a fundamental and unshakable bond and faith between each other. They respect each other, and their deep love for each other would never allow for harmful or abusive behavior.

Draw Up a Love Game Plan

When you identify what needs to change, draw up an action plan for carrying out change. Sometimes external help is advisable, such as a counselor, pastor, or therapist. We've all benefited from a helping hand now and then.

With the help of prayer and meditation, contemplate exactly what you would like in a new love relationship. What are the characteristics you want your new partner to have? Here are some thoughts I've heard from the people I've interviewed:

"Someone I can share the deepest part of me with."

"Someone on the same spiritual path."

"Someone I can communicate with."

"Compassion, harmony, and balance."

"Someone who understands and accepts me."

"Someone who really knows me."

"Someone I can love, and who will love me, without condition or reservation."

"Trust! That's everything."

I seldom hear about sexual passion as a *primary* prerequisite for soulmates. Everyone in search of a soulmate will agree that sexual attraction and passion are important, but they are not the overwhelming factors. "Of course the sex will be great . . ." and "Of course we would have to be very attracted to each other . . ." people will add. Perhaps the downplaying of sex is due to the fact that we've all had relationships that started with a physical bang but couldn't hold together when the red-hot passion slowed down. A love partner relationship cannot thrive and survive on sex alone.

Rather, when we have a deep soul link with someone, the passion is automatically part of the picture.

Another factor I don't often hear cited is "lots of money." Again, people will agree that financial responsibility and security are important, but not more important than other factors. Money doesn't buy happiness. There are plenty of wealthy people who are very lonely. Often money can impede intimacy. You worry whether someone is interested in you because of you or because of your material wealth.

What's high on this list of comments are desires for emotional, mental, and spiritual bonding. A sharing of worldview. A communion of souls in the vast cosmic scheme of things. When emotional, mental, and spiritual intimacy take place, they ignite and enhance physical passion. Nurtured and nourished, we feel comfortable in the vulnerability of love and sex.

When I faced looking for a new partner myself, my highest priority was that he and I would share the same fundamental spiritual path—that we would be on the same wavelength. I decided that I would rather be alone than not have that rapport.

People look for soulmates when they've had the spiritual side of them awaken. They yearn for something that goes beyond the bread and butter of everyday life.

List the characteristics you'd like in a soulmate. Write them quickly, without judging them. Be as specific as you'd like.

In another list, state how you want to be loved, and how you want to love in return. Again, be very specific.

Go over the lists and prioritize what you have written. Balance your idealism with realism. If you create a picture that no one could possibly match, you won't have much success. Emphasize inner qualities over external things. Inner strength and virtues have staying power. External things—like money—can disappear. Cross off whatever is not appropriate.

Save the final lists. They will become your working blueprint.

Specific versus general

Some people feel that lists potentially limit options, and that it is better to be general and open-ended. The same debate has occurred over prayer. Is it better to envision and ask for specifics or simply to envision and ask for whatever is best?

Neither method is better than the other; they both work equally well. Studies of general and directed prayer, for example, have shown both to be effective. The answer lies in the preference of the individual. Some people feel more comfortable asking only for their "highest good" on the premise that they may not be able to perceive what that might be. They trust that the right answer will be delivered.

Other people feel more comfortable putting together specifics. I'm definitely in this camp. I feel that if I am not specific, the universe will randomly fill in the blanks, and I may get something other than what I'd like. Of course, those who favor generalities would say that this is what I am meant to have.

I believe that the divine gift of free will means that we are meant to be active participants in the creation of our reality. Otherwise, we are merely passive recipients. Manifestation is a partnership between humanity and God. We must use our will to help bring things into manifestation. We each bear the responsibility of directing our will to the highest purpose, and not to selfish ends.

Our thought, intent, and will have great power to organize forces in the universe. One can be focused and yet open to possibilities as well. When we stay focused on spiritual qualities, the material things work out accordingly.

Specifics enable us to craft a vision. A vision takes on a tangible form and helps us to direct our energy and resources toward achieving what we desire. Top athletes know that winning is more than just skill and expertise; it requires a very specific vision of their goal.

Consequently, when envisioning a soulmate relationship, it is important to be as specific as you can be within your zone of comfort. Think of specifics as an outline. Hold the expectation that the outline will be filled in according to the highest good.

The following chapters will help you hone your vision and put it into action.

8

Listen to Your Intuition

*God knows all things perfectly at the same moment by
a single, simple intuition.*

—Saint Robert Bellarmine

First and foremost, manifesting your soulmate involves inner work, and that requires intuition. Everyone has intuition; it's an inner compass, a guidance system, that everyone is born with. Intuition is that part of us that is Higher Self or our connection to God or the Universal Mind, which is able to scan beyond our limited sense of time and space. It is like a giant radar sweep that constantly searches out the best path, the best opportunities, the best way to achieve love and wholeness. Our intuition provides unfailing guidance that helps us make the best decisions, stay on a smooth course, and unfold our greatest purpose and good.

Your own intuition functions all the time. Perhaps you are not always aware of it. Your gut feelings and hunches are your intuition speaking to you. If you feel that something is right or wrong without being able to explain precisely why, your intuition has given you a heads up.

Intuition uses many ways to get guidance across to us. Most common are signs in the body, such as the gut feeling, or tingling of the skin, or a buzzing in the ears. Also common are emotions: we get strong feelings, good or bad, in reaction to something. We may also hear an authoritative voice inside our head, or even in the space around us, that seems different than our usual inner mental talk. We may experience a knowing, simply a certainty about the truth of something.

Intuition also speaks to us through our dreams. If you work with your dreams, you will receive valuable guidance and information. Chapter 14 goes into more detail about how to use your dreams to find your soulmate.

And, intuition delivers information to us through synchronicity—being guided to the right place at the right time without knowing it beforehand—and through things people say to us and things we read and come upon.

The universe is constantly organizing toward wholeness. Thus the world can be your blackboard of messages that are meaningful to you.

But guidance from intuition will not help if you do not listen and do not act. If you have asked to meet your soulmate, and you are prompted to take a certain course of action, follow it.

The more you pay attention to your intuition and act upon it, the stronger it gets. It's often easy to dismiss intuition as imagination. But if you listen to it, you will discover that it is unfailing in its good guidance.

Intuition guides us on matters both small and large. It can help us avoid delays, and it can help us navigate major changes in life.

In the following story, Helene followed her intuition as it

guided her around the world and to the man who was her soulmate.

I was fifteen years old, depressed about not having a boyfriend, by
myself in my room, when I heard my Higher Self tell me that I would
travel to a foreign country and meet my soulmate there. At the time
I was living in Buenos Aires, Argentina, and was in high school. As I
always trusted my inner voice, I began saving money during the
summer to travel and began telling people that I would travel to a
foreign country. When asked where, I would say either Spain, the
United States, England, or Germany because I spoke Spanish and
German and was learning English in high school. I deeply trusted my
intuition and Higher Self, even though I did not confide to anybody
that I had a voice that spoke to me inside my head.

I graduated from high school and began working during the
day and going to the University of Buenos Aires during the
evenings. At the university I saw a woman that lived in the general
neighborhood I lived in. She had attended a German private
school while I had gone to a public school. I felt she was snobbish
because she always had been disdainful to me. But here we were,
both intimidated by these big walls and rooms, knowing not a
soul, so when we saw each other, we greeted each other like long-
lost friends. We began traveling home in the train together.

I found out her parents were moving to the United States, but
she did not want to go. The moment she mentioned it, I knew this
is where I was supposed to go. B. had a boyfriend and wanted to
marry him. She also was born in Argentina and felt very consonant
with the culture. Her mother wanted to travel to the U.S. because
her half sister was divorcing there and her father was in the mood
to travel to another culture.

I immediately offered for her to live with us (without consulting with my parents) until we both graduated and told her that if by then she had not married, I would go with her to the U.S. I told my parents about it. They were not too happy about it, but they agreed to meet her parents. Her parents were happy that an interim solution to the problem had been found.

So her parents left for the U.S.A., and B. moved in with us. We had two years until graduation. Her relationship with her boyfriend deteriorated, as he was not ready for marriage, and she began joining my friends and planning our trip to the U.S.A.

By the time we left, B. was twenty-one years old, and her parents had to find her a job in order for her to have a permanent green card. They found us both jobs with friends of theirs, to mentor children and teach them languages. We both graduated and left for California with green cards in our hands.

We lived with her parents for a year, traveled to Europe for three months, and then settled into our own apartment in Hollywood.

There I met Victor. I did not like him at all. He was loud, outgoing, and aggressively pursuing me. He was forty-two years old, twice divorced, and going through midlife crisis. I was twenty-two by then, and my idea of my soulmate was that he would be tall, blond, and have a successful career and life. Victor was shorter than I was and balding. I was quite introverted and not very social. After a couple of months, and because I was not dating anybody at the time, I went on a date with him. He danced with B. all night long—they both were very good dancers—and I sat sedately with B.'s boyfriend, wondering what the heck I was doing there.

When we went home, we had a cup of coffee and we began talking. We talked for four hours. Victor showed a side of him not visible in his public person. Privately he was serious, a deep thinker and philosopher and the first man with whom I was able to have a deep and satisfying conversation in my life. We began dating.

Once Victor showed his private self, I felt like I had known him all my life. I was deeply comfortable with him. My sexuality bloomed. Because he was surrounded by all these books trying to sort out who he was, I was exposed, for the first time in my life, to the psychology of the late sixties. Every book he read, I read. We discussed who we were and what our dreams were. It was all deeply nourishing. I went back to school, as I felt psychology was one of my loves. We would study together, then eat, then make love. We were filled with each other and our long conversations.

Even though it all felt so right from the inside, I was very young and had serious doubts about committing to Victor. He wanted to get married. I was nowhere ready. He also suffered from epilepsy. So here was a man with whom I could do anything that nourished my body and soul but was nineteen years older than me, had epilepsy, had been married twice before, had very little money, and was changing the direction of his work.

I decided to date other men and stay as friends. He tried to commit suicide but called me after ingesting a bottle of pills. It was the strangest experience, but when I finally saw him in the hospital bed, after having his stomach pumped out, I felt like he had dropped further masks, and I saw him very deeply, like I was seeing his soul.

But my ambivalence continued, particularly because he had tried to kill himself. He recuperated and went back to work. We stayed friends throughout. By the time I was twenty-eight, and after dating various men, I realized that this was my soulmate. I may have preferred that he be younger, healthier, richer, and more handsome, but the reality was that this was the man with whom all of me hummed.

I made a commitment to live together. I still could not commit to marriage. We moved in together when I was twenty-eight, and I had a major spiritual opening. After that, I knew we would stay together. We were doing some very deep work, healing our childhood wounds of intimacy and our love was growing. When I was thirty-two, I was finally ready to marry, and I proposed. We wrote our own ceremony and were married in our living room, in the company of a nondenominational minister and two very dear friends. It was the most beautiful day of my life. The sun shone brightly, and everything went according to God's plan.

I am now fifty-five years old and he is seventy-four. We went through some very dark times for seven years when I was forty-one years old. We came through stronger and with a deeper love and commitment. We decided against having children because of his health and our age difference, and that was painful. Yet our love grows stronger and our spirit brighter. He is experiencing illness due to the medicine that he has to take for his condition. Yet last year he committed to healing and finding new ways because we both want more years together. We are doing the necessary work in our relationship to create that new beginning. Our relationship has developed a life of its own. Sometimes I trust it more than I trust our individual process.

When we first met, Victor had a dream that we would work together. I could never envision that because of our deep cultural and individual differences. Now that is becoming part of our dream, after thirty-two years. The strange thing about us was that from the outside we always were very different, not only physically, but in our temperaments and inclinations. Yet underneath there always was this strong bond that we both could rely on. He approached the world from the outside in, I approached the world from the inside out. Just the beginning of this year we felt like we were crossing over into each other's territory.

There was so much love between us always, no matter what. Our hearts talked to each other even when differences surfaced and created problems.

Helene might have ignored the message from her Higher Self that she would go to a foreign country and meet her soulmate there. It could easily have been regarded as a daydream fantasy. But, without knowing exactly how or when, she put her faith in the unfoldment of that path. She allowed circumstances to arrange themselves as necessary. She also galvanized the unfoldment through her actions of saving money and telling others what she intended to do. Thus, she focused her intent, which organized universal forces on her behalf, and she affirmed her intent through her words.

Helene acknowledged that at first Victor didn't meet her vision of a soulmate. It is possible that her vision was based on wishful thinking. But, once again, she was guided intuitively to look again. Thanks to her intuition, she did not miss her soulmate.

There are many ways to strengthen your intuition, and I have put together a comprehensive, self-guided program in *Breakthrough Intuition: How to Achieve a Life of Abundance by Listening to the Voice Within*. The most effective step you can take is to increase your awareness of body sensations, feelings, and thoughts that arise within you. Helene told me that she felt deeply comfortable in her body concerning Victor. She did not mean this in a sexual way, but in terms of intuition expressed through the body.

Increase your awareness of your environment. Signs, signals, and guidance can come in the form of synchronicities in nature, events, and conversations.

Pay attention to your dreams.

Intuition is spontaneous. Once you have acknowledged the intuition, then trust it and act on it. Intuition requires action in order to fulfill its purpose of guidance for your best interests.

If you practice the techniques in this book, your intuition will naturally benefit. You will see, in the personal experiences described, how people paid attention to their intuition. Like Helene, they sometimes did not know exactly what the intuition was saying or leading them to, but they trusted their inner guidance and followed along.

9
The Art of Manifestation

True love is not in word only but also in action and truth.

—SAINT COLUMBANUS

The intent to find a soulmate sends a signal out into the cosmos. It's important to keep the signal strong and well-focused. The signal acts like a magnet, setting into motion one of the primary metaphysical principles of the cosmos, the law of attraction. According to that law, we draw to us what we think, say, believe, and act upon. Thus, we must use spiritual tools for creating mindfulness about what goes on inside of us, and what we put out into the world in words and deeds.

If you go around joking that you never find a good relationship, you are giving strength and energy to an idea that will, in turn, become a subconscious belief and help your self-deprecating little joke turn into reality. Think, speak, and act responsibly, not only in terms of your relationships, but in all areas of life. Amazing results happen when you lift your consciousness to a higher and more positive level.

Let's consider ways to build your vision and get results.

Emotional Tone

My mystical experience on the beach was preceded by a feeling of complete peace. I was happy and felt part of my surroundings. The success of undertaking the techniques described below will be influenced by your emotional state. Bring as much positive emotional intensity as you can to the experience.

First, practice conjuring up feelings of happiness, peace, and well-being. What does it feel like to be totally happy in every cell of your being? Think of a person, call up a memory.

Prior to doing any of the exercises, prepare yourself by establishing a happy state of consciousness. Hold it throughout the exercise.

Visualization

One of the most powerful tools that athletes use in their training is the visualization of their top, winning performance. They create a strong mental picture of themselves and inject into it as much enthusiasm and intensity as possible. They bring all their senses to bear: They *see* it, *hear* it, *taste* it, *say* it, *touch* it. They put emotion into it: they *feel* it. Every part of their being is directed toward the winning performance.

Such visualization techniques are used by many people to achieve all kinds of goals: test performances, artistic performances, creativity, invention, business successes, salesmanship, motivation, and so on. Top performers know that they must create a mental reality in order to make a physical reality happen.

Visualization is a powerful technique for soulmates, too. Create a mental picture from the specifics you have listed for a soulmate. See yourself enjoying the qualities of the relationship: happiness, love, harmony, domestic tranquillity, recreational activities, and so forth. Put as much color, detail, and emotion into the vision as possible.

As for the soulmate, start with a general picture of a partner. You may find that details spontaneously appear. If so, allow them to become part of the vision. If no details appear, do not try to force any. See your partner in outline or silhouette.

Cathy practiced this visualization:

I love to be out in nature. I especially like taking nature walks and watching birds. I feel closer to God when I do those things. My soulmate would have to like those things, too, because sharing this would bring us closer to each other, and closer together as one to God, as well. It would be one of the important ways we would connect, soul to soul.

Every day, or as often as I could, I would call up a picture of myself and my soulmate in some beautiful outdoor setting. We would take great interest and delight in the flowers and vegetation, the look of the sky, the smell of air. We would point out birds in the trees and in the bushes. I even created conversations between us as we discovered all the treasures around us.

At first, the "mystery man," as I called him, had no face. I almost didn't want to put a face on him; I knew what I wanted *in* him, but didn't want to dictate appearances. But after I'd done this visualization for a while, something strange happened. I still didn't see a face, but I could clearly see a cord of light connecting us through the heart. It was as though we were sort of transparent, except for this cord of light. I could see it penetrating both of us very deeply.

I took this as a sign that though nothing was happening yet in my daily life, something was indeed happening on some other plane. I had a feeling of certainty that this cord would draw us together, and that I would soon meet the man at the other end of it.

I have to admit, though, that I started to get discouraged when several months went by and nothing happened. But whenever I started to feel low, I would think of that cord of light connecting us through the hearts, and I would be encouraged not to give up. I reminded myself that finding this person would happen on its own timetable when the circumstances were right.

When I finally met Kevin, I was very attracted to him and felt a special sort of energy or aura around him. When he mentioned that he was a birder, I felt a zing go through me, and I knew I had finally found the man in my vision. I feel we are connected soul to soul through the heart, just as I'd seen in the visualization.

Cathy started with a picture of sharing. It was both an emotional sharing and a spiritual sharing. Though specific, it focused on a *quality* of the relationship that she wanted. Her intuition added a powerful ingredient with the heart-to-heart cord. It served as validation to Cathy that this desire was right and true for her. It carried with it an intuitive knowing that the relationship she sought would indeed manifest. Thus, it bolstered her faith, which enabled her to continue the visualization as energetically as possible.

Visualization took a different form for Elena. She also experienced a vision that took on a life of its own.

I had a very firm idea of what I wanted to picture about my soul-mate, but when I concentrated on it, it started to change on me. I tried to go back to my original but couldn't stay on it. Finally, I just let the visualization do what it wanted to do. What I saw was nothing but a ball or point of light. It was surrounded by darkness. But far off in the distance was another ball of light. It got closer and closer. I suddenly realized that the ball of light before me was *me,* and that the ball of light coming in from a distance was my soul-mate. The lights seemed to represent us in our true essence. Form didn't seem to matter. I didn't need to be concerned about what he looked like, or anything like that. I just knew that what was coming was right, and I didn't need to worry.

Elena did the right thing by not trying to force the visualization. Rather, she allowed her intuition to change it into an image that would be of the most help to her. The picture we start with is a beginning, and it helps to set forces in motion. If it changes, it guides us to focus our intention even more precisely in the manner that is right for us.

Some visualizations begin with great detail and remain that way, as in the following example from a woman named Joan.

While I was making up a list of all the things I wanted in a soul-mate, I got a very clear picture of him in my mind. It wasn't anyone I knew. Part of me thought that I just made him up, but I had this conviction in the pit of my stomach that this person was real, not a figment of my imagination, and that I would be able to meet him. He was about five nine in height, very lean, with light brown hair that had a certain wave to it. His eyes were greyish light blue. I could see every detail of his face, including a little mole above one brow. Most amazingly, I could smell his skin—it was like salt air, like being at the shore.

About a year went by before I actually met him. Suffice it to say that our meeting was unexpected, and when I saw him, I almost fell over. I thought, "You're the man in my vision!" The details were all accurate, right down to the mole.

Joan may have experienced precognition, a paranormal glimpse into the future. The image of her soulmate presented itself and was not consciously created by her. Joan intuitively gave the image space and energy by keeping it in her visualization.

The esoteric adept and teacher Rudolph Steiner said that mental pictures are important because they become motives for action and "defining patterns for all later decisions." When visualizations become firmly cemented into consciousness, action naturally follows, and what is envisioned becomes reality.

Steiner said that love, apart from being an expression of the sexual drive, "is based on mental pictures that we have formed of the beloved." He went on:

And the more idealistic these mental pictures, the more blessed is the love. Here, too, thought is the father of feeling. People say that love makes us blind to the beloved's flaws. But we can also turn this around and claim that love opens our eyes to the beloved's strengths. Many pass by these good qualities without noticing them. One person sees them and, just for this reason, love awakens in the soul. What else has the person done but make a mental picture of what a hundred others have ignored? Love is not theirs because they lack the *mental picture*.

If we hold vivid mental pictures about love, we find what we picture.

Affirmations

Visualizations can be strengthened with the addition of affirmations, positive statements about realizing things that are yet to be. If the universe can be likened to an ocean of possibilities, then affirmations are the fishing lines we cast in to capture and land the ones we want.

Affirmations assume we already have what we seek. They are based on the metaphysical principle that every soul has its own and rightful supply of good from the unlimited Universal Supply; it's simply a matter of bringing the good into manifestation. Your good does not diminish my good, so one need never worry about getting theirs before someone else does. Translating that to soulmates means that no one is going to grab the person who is meant for you. Soulmates are not prizes in shooting galleries. Consequently, even if your soulmate does not come along quickly, you needn't worry that he or she has been taken on a detour.

An affirmation is simple, clear, and positive:

"I am enjoying my relationship with my soulmate."

"I have found my soulmate."

"I am with my soulmate."

"Love is in divine order in my life."

Adding "now" to the statement asserts that the manifestation is rooted firmly in physical reality. "Now" may help the process along by organizing the forces of the universe more efficiently. Ultimately, however, we meet our soulmates when we are meant to meet them.

It also is a good idea to include gratitude in an affirmation:

"I give thanks for enjoying my relationship with my soulmate."

"I give thanks that I have found my soulmate now."

Gratitude keeps us connected to God or Spirit and reminds us that everything we do is a partnership of the realms of earth and heaven.

Affirmations help us to keep our intent energized and focused and to maintain our faith and perseverance in the event that results do not appear as fast as we'd like.

Like visualizations, affirmations work when they are undertaken with conviction and total belief. If we don't take them seriously, we don't get serious results.

Compose several affirmations to accompany your visualizations. Be spontaneous, and allow your intuition to work for you.

Meditation

Visualizations and affirmations can be undertaken at any time, but one of the best is in the repose of meditation. Spend quiet time in meditation every day. Meditation is a wonderful way to clear the mind and renew spiritual energy. The discipline of mental clearing and stillness is a superb muscle-builder for intuition.

Prior to meditating, build your visualization in your mind as vividly as possible. Repeat your affirmations. Muster an intensity of feeling and hold both picture and affirmation in that space. Then release them, sending them out into the universe. You might imagine them going out like the beams of searchlights, or radio or television broadcast signals, or all-points news bulletins. As they get sent out, know that they will find their targets.

Then sit quietly and empty the mind of thought as much as possible. Let thoughts trickle out of you like water through a sieve. Imagine yourself a chalice or vessel, receiving the bounty of the Universal Supply.

It's important to spend this time in receptivity. Somewhere out there, your soulmate is searching for *you*. A quiet mind is better able to receive the inspirations, intuition, ideas, and guidance that will help you find each other. Sometimes our guidance is subtle and enters on the subconscious level. From there, it reaches conscious thought at the right moment.

Here is Kyle's experience with meditation.

I have been in the habit of meditating for years, so it seemed perfectly natural to meditate to find my soulmate. I would send out my request and then sit quietly for a while. I began getting pictures of what she looked like. I could see the two of us together. One particular image of a café or coffeehouse kept repeating. That puzzled me, because I didn't frequent any place like that.

Then I had to go out of town on business. I was walking down the street after a meeting and passed by this coffeehouse. It looked real appealing. Suddenly it seemed like a good idea to go in and have a drink. At the time, I didn't connect it to my meditation at all. I wasn't even thinking about soulmates—I was still caught up in what had happened in the meeting. Well, as you might guess, that's where I met her! Later it dawned on me that somehow I had been guided to the place I'd seen in my meditation. It wasn't exactly the same, but it was a coffeehouse.

The odd thing was, Paula told me that she had also stopped in on what seemed like a whim. We figured that somehow we were both guided to be there, at that precise spot, at the same time.

The meditation provided a way for Kyle's intuition to give him key guidance on both a conscious and subconscious level. He followed his intuitive prompting to stop at the coffeehouse. Paula also allowed her intuition to take her there.

In the next case, the meditation was not as dramatic, but it led to the right results.

I meditated a lot. I kept it up, even though nothing seemed to happen. Just when I was about ready to give up, I met Aleen. I do feel the meditation had a lot to do with it. I believe that something was going on under the surface that I couldn't feel, but it still worked out.

Sometimes the manner in which the universe brings soulmates together is indeed beyond our immediate understanding. We activate the forces and principles, and then we must trust in an eventual result.

Invoking Spiritual Helpers

Numerous spiritual helpers act as intermediaries between the human realm and God. Such helpers can be petitioned to assist us in the search for a soulmate.

Angels

Perhaps you feel the presence of angels around you. Angels are God's messengers, beings of light who carry prayers to God and the answers back. They intervene in our affairs in appropriate ways. They are not magicians; they do not pull things out of hats. They can be called upon to assist us to find our truth and right path. They can help us set forces in motion and organize them.

Said Chandra:

> I asked my guardian angel to help me find my soulmate. I was really sincere about it. I think that's important—angels can see into your heart. Whenever I meditated or prayed about it, I could feel my angel's presence around me. I knew he was listening to me. I did meet my soulmate, and we are extremely happy together. I know my angel guided me to the right place, and I am very thankful.

Calling upon one's guardian angel—or any angel—is a way of drawing closer to God. Angels help us feel a deeper connection to the divine, which in turn stimulates our own powers of manifestation. We feel that anything can be accomplished in partnership with the divine.

Anna wrote heavenly letters.

I wrote letters to both my soulmate and my guardian angel. I told my soulmate that I loved him and I knew he loved me, and that we would find each other. I asked my guardian angel to help me do this. I wrote the letters over and over again, and in my mind I took them to the cosmic post office and mailed them.

The act of writing down our petitions, intents, and even affirmations serves to bring something into the physical realm of being. Writing sets our intent firmly in consciousness. Creating the written word symbolizes the actual creation of what we seek.

Besides one's personal guardian angel, other angels can be petitioned for help. Haniel is the angel who governs the increase of love and romance. Gabriel is the angel of new beginnings and domestic happiness. Michael is the champion of marriage. And Raphael governs communication and connections.

Spiritual guides

Other intermediaries that function in similar capacities to angels are spiritual guides. These may be enlightened souls, human or otherwise, who interact with us through intuition, prayer, meditation, and dreams. They provide guidance and spiritual instruction and tutoring. One usually becomes aware of guides through time spent in spiritual study and inner work. Animals can be spiritual guides as well, as in the following example.

I have always felt a deep affinity with ravens and consider them to be among my spiritual guides and teachers. They are mysterious birds and symbolize to me the mysteries of the world and spirit. They show up a lot in my meditations and dreams and tell me something I need to know. I have a name for one in particular, but it's a secret name.

When I decided to find my soulmate, I asked this raven to help me, to go out and find him, and come back with information. In my meditation I saw him fly off into the depths of space.

One night I had a dream in which I was in a strange house. The raven came down the chimney. It stood in the fireplace giving me a penetrating look. At the time, I couldn't make any sense out of it and wondered what it was supposed to mean.

A few months later I was invited to a Christmas party. I didn't have an escort—I wasn't even dating anyone—and was feeling sad and lonely about being alone during the holidays. But I decided to go to the party, anyway. There were a lot of people I didn't know there, including a striking man who caught my attention. I had the impression that he was there with a date, and thought to myself, *Of course!* Feeling kind of out of place, I drifted over to the fireplace, which had a nice fire going in it, and consoled myself with my wine.

Suddenly—and I'm not sure how this happened, but you know how people can shift around at a party—the Striking Man was practically at my elbow. He turned to me and said, with this twinkle in his eye, "Are you waiting for Santa Claus?" At that moment I could feel this tremendous jolt of energy go through me. Something happened in the look that passed between us. I knew he could feel it, too. It was like a flood of unspoken words passed between us.

For the rest of the evening, we were absolutely riveted to each other. He was not there with a date but had come with another couple who were friends of his.

That was how I met my soulmate—nine years ago. I figured out the dream, too. The raven came down the chimney *like Santa Claus*. With his penetrating look, he was telling me the timing and place of my soulmate meeting. Even though I didn't consciously understand the message, it obviously registered on my subconscious. It was behind my decision to attend the party and also to stand by the fireplace.

I've often wondered if we would have connected at the party, anyway, even if I had not moved over to the fireplace. Probably so, since I do feel we were meant to come together, but the Force moves in mysterious ways! Another way of reading the dream is to see the raven's coming down the chimney like Santa Claus as a symbol of my receiving the greatest gift I could ever want—the love of my soulmate.

Saints

Saints are looked to by millions of people as powerful intercessors who can be petitioned for help in all matters of life. Saints serve as models of purity, spiritual devotion, and charity. Through their works and holiness in life, they achieve an exalted status after death. From heaven, they continue as servants of God and intercede on behalf of humans.

Holy persons exist in all faiths, but what we call *saint* belongs to the Catholic faith. The Church has formal procedures for recognizing saints, based on thorough examinations of their lives and evidence of miracles performed from beyond the grave. The

Church has many saints who achieved their status prior to the institution of these procedures, either through martyrdom—dying for the faith—or through popular acclaim.

People of all faiths petition saints. I believe strongly in the communion of saints, as well as the presence of angels and spiritual guides. We have many choices in our spiritual helpers.

Many people feel a close association with a patron saint, who, similar to a guardian angel, has a special relationship with a person. Saints also have their specific patronages, which usually have a bearing on their lives and works. In matters of love and romance, Saint Valentine, the namesake of Valentine's Day, is the patron saint.

Little is known about the real Valentine, a physician who died ca. 269 or 270. Most probably, he either lived in Rome or was called from Terni to Rome as a consequence of his aid to Christian martyrs. There are different versions of his fate, likely more legend than fact. In one, he was arrested and jailed. When he refused to renounce his faith, he was beaten and beheaded on February 14. Legend has it that on the morning of his execution, he supposedly sent a farewell message to the jailer's daughter, signed "from your Valentine."

Another legend holds that he was arrested for assisting couples to get married, which displeased Emperor Claudius II. Valentine was not executed but died in prison.

Such stories—that Valentine helped lovers and that he sent loving messages—have connected the saint with romance. Other sources of the connection between Valentine's date of martyrdom and love stem from early Roman festivals, such as *Lupercalia,* which involved young noblemen running through the streets with goatskin thongs while the young women tried to lash the thongs and thereby improve their chances at child-bearing. The thongs were called *februa,* and the lashing *februatio,* from a Latin word meaning "to purify," the same root as February. In other celebrations, Roman men drew names of available young ladies out of a box and promised to love them—at least until the festival next year.

The custom of giving flowers for Valentine's Day supposedly began with a daughter of King Henry IV of France, who threw a party to honor the saint and gave every lady present a bouquet.

Another saint who may be petitioned regarding soulmates is Joseph, the father of Jesus, who is the patron saint of families. His help may be particularly valuable to single parents who wish to establish family harmony and happiness as part of their soulmate connection.

If you feel a kinship with saints—or would like to establish one—bring them into your prayer and meditation.

Getting validation

Spiritual helpers can be asked to validate guidance and feelings, as well as for assistance in meeting our soulmate. We often want reassurances that we haven't fantasized or read signals the wrong way. I asked for validation of my mystical experience at the beach and received it in the form of significant objects I found there on my walks.

When Sophie met her soulmate, it seemed almost too good to be true, and so she asked for validation.

One day, when he left my apartment, I watched him leave, walking in the courtyard, and I carefully looked at his back. I know that when you look at people's backs you very clearly see things you don't see when you're facing them. Then I asked my guides, or my angels, or whomever: "Now tell me truly and honestly, is this man the love of my life?" The answer was like a quiet and steady voice murmuring in my ear: "Yes, he is." There could have been a different answer and I would have accepted it, I am sure. For I've been in love before, and although I would be very anxious to get a positive answer, I would always hear "No" when I asked that question.

When we ask for spiritual counsel, we must be willing to accept the answer that is given, even if it is not the one we want. The voice of spirit uses our intuition to speak to us. The true answer comes spontaneously.

In the next chapters, we will explore more ways to do inner work for manifesting a soulmate relationship.

10

Soulmates and the Seven Chakras

My heart leaps up when I behold
A rainbow in the sky.

—William Wordsworth

A soulmate relationship is a fundamentally harmonious union of body, mind, and soul. We certainly want to have a pleasurable and passionate sexual life. We want a partner who thinks along the same lines as we do, or at least understands or accepts what we think. And we want to feel a deep spiritual bond.

In previous chapters, we've discussed the cords of universal life energy that connect us to other souls from life to life; Cindy's visualization showed such a cord of light connecting her and her soulmate through the heart.

Cords of life energy radiate out from all our chakras. Chakras are wheel-shaped interfaces that funnel the universal life energy into the body and the auric envelope around it. There are hundreds of chakras throughout the body, and seven primary ones that are aligned approximately along the spinal column, from the root, or base of the spine, to the crown, or top of the head.

Each chakra governs a different aspect of life, as well as different physical and psychospiritual functions. The chakras are increasingly complex the farther up the column they are. Each has a different color and number of spokes or petals to its wheel. The wheels rotate. When chakras are well-balanced, they rotate smoothly and their color is clear; our total body-mind-soul health is benefited.

The chakras link our body to the auric envelope around it. The aura has different layers; most healers and clairvoyants identify seven, which in turn relate to the seven primary chakras. Each is more subtle the farther away it is from the physical body. The aura has no finite boundary but becomes finer and finer as it extends into infinite space.

The energy of the aura is explained in mystical traditions as a subtle force that goes beyond the realm of matter. The aura has actually been measured by a device called the eclectromyogram (EMG), originally used to measure the electrical activity in muscles. Valerie Hunt, a physical therapist and professor of kinesiology at the University of California, has detected electrical frequencies much more subtle than traditional body frequencies radiating from the chakra points.

I learned how to perceive the chakras by developing my intuition and studying energy healing. When I clairvoyantly see an aura, I am drawn to certain chakras that are in need of balancing. I may get impressions of how the chakra is blocked or clogged, as well as emotional and karmic baggage floating there. Old wounds and unresolved issues remain in our energy fields.

I also may see how thoughts and belief patterns are manifesting. Thought creates reality; we become what we think, and we attract to us what we think. If you want to change your outer house, you have to first set your inner house in order.

Ideally, a strong love relationship will have vibrant energy cords in all seven primary chakras. Here is a summary of the chakras and how they figure in our relationships.

First chakra (root)

COLOR: RED

The root chakra encompasses the most basic level of life. Our focus here is on maintaining the physical body and gaining a foothold in the material world. Our needs for food, shelter, and clothing drive us. We want security, safety, and stability. We are concerned with the physical plane of existence.

We are conditioned by our environment—our family, cultural, ethnic, and racial expectations. Here we also find our core beliefs and code of honor: our view of how the world ought to treat us, what we deserve, and how we should get what we deserve. Such conditioning is crucial, for it affects our outlook throughout life and how successful we are likely to be in achieving our goals and desires.

At the root chakra, a partner is evaluated based on his or her ability to provide the basics for survival. We temper the evaluation with our conditioning. Perhaps our family or culture has certain expectations—or even makes certain demands—upon who we will have as a partner and how the choice will be made.

In many societies today, marriages are still arranged by parents. Higher-chakra functions such as love and spiritual bonding don't enter into the equation. Marriages are treated more like business partnerships, forged to bring advantage to a larger corporate entity.

Even when marriages are not arranged, tribal expectations can still bring great pressure to the selection process for a partner. You might be expected to marry within your race, class, or social standing. Your parents might want you to marry a person whose profession will bring respect and money.

The younger you are, the more vulnerable you are to tribal expectations, and thus the more likely you are to let first chakra factors dictate finding a partner. I have seen many older persons, however, still trapped in old conditioning that no longer serves them.

You are also more likely to make a first chakra choice if you are desperately trying to escape from an undesirable situation, such as an unhappy homelife. A person who offers security, safety, and stability may seem like the ideal mate. But the idealism will not last if there is little or no union between the upper chakras.

We are best able to make a first chakra evaluation when we feel secure, safe, and stable in our own right. If we can provide for our own basic needs, we can see a potential partner in an equal light.

Second chakra (spleen)
COLOR: ORANGE

The second or spleen chakra holds our sexual energy, our instincts and passions, and our desire to attract and possess both people and things. The spleen chakra is linked to the lower astral plane of instincts.

We may mistake a tremendous, even insatiable, physical attraction as soulmate passion. True soulmate passion is fired in all seven chakras. When it resides primarily in the spleen chakra, the physical thrill eventually wears off and the passion diminishes over time. If the other bondings are not sufficient, an emptiness sets in that penetrates to the upper levels.

Spleen chakra energy is assertive. We need it to make our way in the world, to forge ahead, to take risks. Spleen chakra energy also is controlling. Money, power, possessions, and people can all become pawns to serve our passions and desires. We define ourselves by what we have.

Many people get stuck in second chakra issues. The advertising, media hype, and consumerism of Western society feed this body relentlessly, telling us that we are nothing without possessions. We are told that our happiness depends upon the beautiful partner, the huge bank account, the big house, the late model car, and so on. We engage in power struggles and manipulation to feed the addiction.

A second chakra relationship is giddy for a time, but the boom eventually busts. The sexual and material spending exhaust the spiritual bank account.

Second chakra harmony exists when both partners are on an equal footing with each other. They enjoy a good sexual relationship that is a giving and receiving of pleasure as part of the love they express for each other. They are in agreement about material things in their life and share the same comfort zone with regard to spending, saving, and acquiring possessions.

Third chakra (solar plexus)

COLOR: YELLOW

Emotions, feelings of attraction, and desire for union are uppermost in the third chakra. It corresponds to the upper astral plane, which contains our self-esteem, inner power, sense of responsibility, and honesty.

Many people become mired in third or solar plexus chakra issues, too. Low self-esteem can drive an obsessive emotional need to be loved, though this kind of love is demanding, controlling, and capricious. A desire to be in a marriage or partnership simply for the sake of the union, or to avoid being alone, can blind us to the right choices.

A woman once told me that she had been praying for a husband for three years. None had materialized in that time, and she was about to give up on prayer. She felt that God wasn't listening, or worse, that he had abandoned her. "Prayer doesn't work," she said. "At least it doesn't work for me."

As we talked, it became evident to me that this woman was so intent upon Having A Husband that just about any candidate would do. It was probably fortunate that no one had proposed, otherwise she might have made a mistake she would later regret. God *was* listening to her and was watching out for her, though in ways she could not recognize.

I said to her, "Do you want just any man for a husband, or do you want the man who is right and ideal for you?"

She affirmed that she wanted the right and ideal man.

"Then you should continue your prayers for that man, and be confident that you will meet him when the time is right for both of you."

Waiting for the right partner can be hard to do. When we have a void in life, we want to fill it. If we are alone, it seems the entire world is paired off in couples. It's important to remember the spiritual law of attraction: We receive what we believe. If we send a message of emotional neediness out into the universe, our call will be answered by those who need an emotionally dependent person. Such a relationship has an imbalance of power. Without growth, it is unlikely to rise to the heights of true and pure love.

When our third chakra is balanced, we know our emotions with great honesty, and we know the basis for our attraction to someone. We are able to observe, know, and accept their flaws, as they do in us. Above all, we have self-esteem: We are comfortable with ourselves and confident in our gifts that we have to offer to another.

Fourth chakra (heart)
COLOR: GREEN

Many of us spend our entire lives in relationships that revolve around the lower three chakras. When the higher spiritual centers open, love and relationships are seen in a new light. The desire for a deeper love is born. Sometimes the existing partnerships grow and evolve into the higher spiritual centers. Sometimes they do not, and relationships come apart. Spiritually awakened people look for new partners who meet certain spiritual criteria. Often, an earlier emphasis on money, power, and status take a backseat to new areas that are now more important for soul satisfaction.

The fourth or heart chakra concerns love, understanding, forgiveness, compassion, nurturing and selflessness. It encompasses the lower level of the mental plane, which concerns memory and concrete thinking. The fourth chakra lies between the lower three chakras and the upper three chakras, and thus is the turning point. It isn't that we do not love in the lower three chakras. We do, but our ideas about love are more limited. When the heart center fully awakens to love, we have an awareness of a bigger picture, an awareness that is much more subtle and refined.

We can love deeply from the heart without loving unconditionally. When we learn what is unconditional love, life changes profoundly. We learn about unconditional love through loving and through our spiritual growth.

True love is not romantic love, though romantic love is a part of it. True love is not sexual passion, though sexual passion is a part of it. True love is selfless, never possessive. It spreads beyond the relationship itself to the more vast and more cosmic scheme of things, to love on all levels, including divine love.

Sometimes we equate true love with putting up with another's transgressions and abuses. It's one thing to forgive a mistake—we all make them—and quite another to endure a constant pattern of negative behavior. Then we are not participating in true love but in a power struggle born out of the lower chakras.

True love helps to liberate us from the confines of the lower bodies and energizes and fertilizes the upper chakras.

Fifth chakra (throat)
COLOR: BLUE

The fifth or throat chakra takes us into the upper mental plane, into abstract thought and contemplation. The throat center expresses our will and creativity. This is not the give-it-to-me will of the second chakra but the will that comes from our purpose in life, from the deep expression of who we are as souls as well as personalities.

We can be stifled in this creative expression of will early in life by the root chakra expectations imposed on us by others. We can also be stifled by second and third chakra power and emotional games.

Soulmate love releases the energy of the fifth chakra like a dove. It enables us to flower, to create, to bring into being. We are free from fear of ridicule or censure.

But while we are growing individually, the soulmate relationship develops a mutual voice, the expression of combined energies, united souls. We sing our own song out into the universe, and we also sing a love duet.

The singing of this duet sends out a powerful force. It is a harmony of masculine and feminine that becomes the harmony of the Divine Masculine and Divine Feminine.

Sixth chakra (brow)
COLOR: VIOLET

The sixth or brow chakra—also called the third eye—centers onto the lower spiritual plane of consciousness. The brow chakra has to do with the opening of our psychic senses and spiritual vision. Here is the center of faith: We see the unseen, the potential, and know that we can bring it into manifestation. We see into the realms of spirit; we understand mystical subtleties that go beyond the description of words. The sixth spiritual plane opens the path to Oneness.

In the sixth chakra, we learn detachment. This doesn't mean that we cease loving or needing someone. Rather, we free ourselves from need, and in that freedom, love expands.

The sixth chakra is concerned with learning the big picture—the relationship of the soul to God, and to the All That Is. We gain a sense of our immortality, of past lives, of destinies woven together time after time. The karmic bonds to others are understood here in the sixth chakra. A relationship of deep love serves the path to Oneness. Emotions, love, and sexual expression all take on a higher vibration. We feel merged together at a level of soul as well as body and mind.

Seventh chakra (crown)
COLOR: INDIGO

The seventh or crown chakra reaches into the upper spiritual plane, where exist pure spirit, absolute harmony, and Oneness. In mystical traditions, the opening of the crown chakra brings enlightenment and the experience of the boundless Oneness. Here all things flow back to the One. There is no more *I* or *we*. The seventh chakra corresponds to the seventh spiritual plane of Oneness, which Dion Fortune described as the "All are One and One is All."

Few relationships can sustain such lofty heights, but we all have glimpses of it. To experience Oneness while still in the physical body helps the soul tremendously between incarnations, enabling the next incarnation to embody a much higher spiritual vibration. As soulmates, we give ourselves to help each other back to God.

Evaluating Relationships

We've all had relationships that revolve around the lower three chakras. Some of those relationships are intense, and we mistake the intensity for true love. We have to open up our own higher spiritual centers in order to understand what a truly spiritual love relationship is all about. Prayer, meditation, and spiritual study are the best ways to develop yourself spiritually.

When the higher centers open, we want a partner who is also open on those same levels. Soul-to-soul lovers meet each other as equals in as many of the seven chakras as possible. You especially must have some rapport in the higher bodies.

You can assess a relationship simply by asking yourself some questions in relation to each of the chakras/planes. Even a strong relationship is not going to be flawless and perfect. There still will be conflicts. We come together in an incarnation in order to help each other to grow and to learn from each other. A love relationship ultimately builds and nurtures, never tears down or destroys.

Questions to Ask

FIRST CHAKRA QUESTIONS:

What are my basic needs, and how will they be met with this person?

What are the expectations of others in my choice of partner?

How much am I influenced by the expectations of others?

What are my own expectations for a partner?

SECOND CHAKRA QUESTIONS:

Does sex dominate the relationship or cloud things I'd rather not notice?

Do either one of us play power games?

Do we agree about money, how to save it and how to spend it?

Do we like the same material surroundings?

THIRD CHAKRA QUESTIONS:

Am I attracted to this person because he/she relieves my loneliness?

Can I objectively see all the pluses and minuses in this person?

How can I honestly describe my self-esteem?

FOURTH CHAKRA QUESTIONS:

How do I describe the love in this relationship?

Are there conditions placed upon love by either party? What are they?

How does the love help both of us to grow and thrive?

FIFTH CHAKRA QUESTIONS:

How does this love enable me to grow and express myself in different ways?

Do I ever feel constrained to "be me" in this relationship?

Is my self-expression part of my spiritual unfoldment?

How does this relationship express a "we" voice?

SIXTH CHAKRA QUESTIONS:

What are the karmic ties between us?

What spiritual lessons have we taught each other?

What spiritual lessons do we still have to teach each other?

How does this relationship foster both our individual and collective spiritual growth?

Are our spiritual outlooks compatible?

SEVENTH CHAKRA QUESTIONS:

How does this relationship help me and our spiritual awakening?

Does this relationship help to deepen my understanding of Truth?

How am I helping my partner's spiritual awakening?

Rainbow Chakra Balancing Exercise

As part of our overall body-mind-soul health program, it's a good idea to pay attention to your chakras. Periodic meditation and visualization work helps to keep them balanced and open. When you are balanced and open on all levels of your being, you are better able to attract the relationships you desire.

You may have noticed in the descriptions of the chakras that their colors form a rainbow. The rainbow is the spectrum of white light broken down into different wavelengths. Combined, the wavelengths merge into the white light of Oneness. The rainbow literally is a path to the One.

The following is a simple exercise of visualization utilizing the image of the rainbow that will gently stimulate and refresh the chakras and prepare a path to your destined lover. You may find yourself receiving intuitive information and insights as you go along. Keep a journal handy so that you can record your thoughts after the exercise is done. (If you are interested in delving more deeply into the chakras, I recommend *Wheels of Life* by Anodea Judith.)

For the exercise:

Play some soft, meditational music. Offer a prayer:

Dear Creator, help me to shine with clear, spiritual light.

Now get seated or lie in a comfortable position. Breathe deeply to relax. Feel all of the stress going out of you. Visualize a stream of white light entering through the top of your head and exiting through your feet into the earth. You are now connected to the spiritual realm and to the physical realm.

You are now ready to work on the chakras. Spend several minutes at each level.

Place your attention on the first or root chakra. See it and feel it as a ball of warm red light. Allow the red light to radiate into your entire body, until it fills every cell. Become bathed in red light. Breathe in red light. Know that the red vibrations heal and nourish you.

Move your attention to the second or spleen chakra. See it and feel it as a ball of warm orange light. Allow the orange light to radiate into your entire body, until it fills every cell. Become bathed in orange light. Breathe in orange light. Know that the orange vibrations heal and nourish you.

Move your attention to the third or solar plexus chakra. See it and feel it as a ball of yellow light. Allow the yellow light to radiate into your entire body, until it fills every cell. Become bathed in yellow light. Breathe in yellow light. Know that the yellow vibrations heal and nourish you.

Move your attention to the fourth or heart chakra. See it and feel it as a ball of green light. Allow the green light to radiate into your entire body, until it fills every cell. Become bathed in green light. Breathe in green light. Know that the green vibrations heal and nourish you.

Move your attention to the fifth or throat chakra. See it and feel it as a ball of blue light. Allow the blue light to radiate into your entire body, until it fills every cell. Become bathed in blue light. Breathe in blue light. Know that the blue vibrations heal and nourish you.

Move your attention to the sixth or brow chakra. See it and feel it as a ball of violet light. Allow the violet light to radiate into your entire body, until it fills every cell. Become bathed in violet light. Breathe in violet light. Know that the violet vibrations heal and nourish you.

Move your attention to the seventh or crown chakra. See it and feel it as a ball of indigo light. Allow the indigo light to radiate into your entire body, until it fills every cell. Become bathed in indigo light. Breathe in indigo light. Know that the indigo vibrations heal and nourish you.

Now unite all of the colors within you so that you become a living, vibrant rainbow of light. The colors are clear and sparkling, alive with their own music. The rainbow extends out from you into infinity, connecting you to the All That Is.

Affirm to yourself: "I attract to me the treasure of love, harmony, wholeness, abundance, and prosperity, all the good that is meant for me. I give love and I receive love. I give thanks for the bounty that is mine."

Remain in this radiant state of expanded consciousness as long as you can. Then breathe deeply and recenter your consciousness in your body. Feel the breath flowing through your body. Push your breath out through your feet, grounding you to the earth. When you are ready, open your eyes, refreshed. Record your thoughts and insights.

This is an excellent exercise for conditioning your consciousness to attract the rewarding love that is meant for you.

11

In the Flow

Heaven's net is indeed vast.
Though its meshes are wide,
it misses nothing.

—LAO-TZU

Everything in the universe is energy. The energy can assume any form and become organized into patterns, such as the physical realm. Matter is energy. Consciousness is energy. Our thoughts and feelings are energy. Creativity is energy. The essence of the soul is energy.

The energies of the universe are in constant motion and interplay. As energies affect each other, they change form. In this fashion, our reality is created. As we saw in the previous chapters, we are the cocreators of our reality, making it and changing it by what we think, say, and do.

To find our partner, we seek to create a new reality for ourselves: one in which we receive and give the perfect love, which in turn helps to create a new stream of life energy.

The basis of affirmations, visualization, and prayers seems simple on the surface. Affirm, visualize, and pray for what you want, and it will materialize. Actually, the process is a bit more complex. If every thought, mental image, prayer, and action created change in the physical plane, our reality would be topsy-turvy all the time.

The universe is a mighty current of energy that represents the whole. It constantly moves toward a state of perfection, which is harmony and balance of the whole. Love is an expression of that harmony, balance, and wholeness. In order to influence the mighty currents, we need to raise our energy—our vibrations—to harmonize with the whole. That's what happened to me on the beach at Manzanita, when I felt myself suspended in the Eternal Now.

We don't have to wait for mysterious forces of nature to converge to experience such states of consciousness. We can create them ourselves by learning to act as a form of energy.

Seeing Yourself As Energy

When I learned energy healing, I studied a variety of methods that involved perception of and manipulation of the body's subtle energy field, or aura. All methods of energy healing share some common fundamentals. The energy of God, the universal life force, exists in all creation and part of it is our own energy field. It is the source of all healing, all creation, and all being. Another term for this energy is the unconditional love of God.

The universal life force is available to us all the time. The more we absorb it, the more it benefits us, not only in health but in all facets of life. We can diminish its flow to us through negativity: anger, fear, unresolved emotion, low self-esteem, etc.

How much the flow is diminished determines the ultimate state of our well-being. When we think and do loving things, we literally are in the light; the universal life force pours through us, radiating out to touch others as well.

The more I studied, the more subtle became my awareness of the universal energy and of a person's energy field. I began to see people not so much as bodies of flesh but as patterns of energy. Clairvoyantly, this looks to me like patterns of colored lights and lines of light. Each person has a unique pattern, much like a fingerprint is unique. It might be arranged in a grid or in swirls, for example. As energy blueprints, we are quite beautiful! You might think of yourself as a living rainbow. The rainbow, remember, is the bridge to heaven. As souls, we are the living energy links between the realm of spirit and the realm of matter.

The energy of our auric blueprint is in constant motion, interacting with the flow, lines, and patterns of the energy of the cosmos. It changes shape, texture, density, and color depending on a variety of factors, such as emotions, health, thoughts, and activity. Certain things bring our energy frequency down. If we are in a bad mood, angry, or depressed, we generate lower energies. The same happens if we are preoccupied with material pursuits at the expense of our spiritual side. When we are up, happy, and loving, and are spiritually centered, we generate higher frequencies.

These energies move out from us and into infinite space. They attract to them similar energies. Whenever we meet someone, our energy fields interact. When we are happy and buoyant, we do not want to be around someone who is angry. If we wish to attract a loving soulmate, we must pay attention to the energy we are generating. Do little self-checks on your mood and thoughts throughout the day. You will catch the low frequencies and be able to replace them with more positive energy.

Sometimes the auric field becomes sluggish or blocked. For example, I often see blockages in the chakras that are related to unresolved emotion or unhealed emotional wounds. These impressions come to me in a variety of ways through the psychic sense. Sometimes I "see" or "feel" blockages. I might see a cloudy area or a color that seems off. I feel thicknesses, ripples, jagged edges, congealed areas, hot areas, and cold areas. Sometimes I see images in the aura that are either like still photographs or symbols, or active like movies. Sometimes I "hear" words, and sometimes I receive an overall "knowing" impression. It doesn't matter whether I have my physical eyes open or closed (I can concentrate on subtleties better with them closed), or if the person is in the same room with me or thousands of miles away. Remember, consciousness is nonlocal, our energies extend into infinite space, and everything exists in the Eternal Now. Energetically, we can meet and mingle across time and space! You've already seen examples of that earlier.

Occasionally when I have worked with a person, I have seen two patterns of energy. One is the existing pattern. The other, superimposed over it, is a potential pattern, which always looks brighter and fresher. It represents something that can come into being if certain choices or actions are taken. These might include dumping inner baggage no longer needed, getting out of a stressful job, or boosting self-esteem. People seek intuitive readings or healing work when they feel they must make positive changes in their lives, but then they protest that they can't take the steps to do so! They've always got a list of reasons why they are trapped. They want the great love of their lives to magically appear, yet they will not take steps to help bring it about.

We can always find ways to make changes for the better. First, we have to make a heartfelt commitment to change—change that is in the highest good. We will always receive guidance for what to do to bring it about. Then we must do the work to bring it about.

My perception of people as patterns of energy has helped me greatly in my own manifestation work. In meditation, I see myself as a flow of light energy that merges with other energies, including the energies of whatever it is I am seeking to bring into my life. I have found this approach to be highly effective, especially when combined with the visualization, affirmation, and prayer techniques of the previous chapters.

To help you get started, let's work first with achieving familiarity with your own energy pattern. Allow impressions to arise spontaneously. Some people will have more visual impressions, while others will have feelings, or even experience energy as sound.

For each of the meditation exercises in this chapter, prepare yourself by relaxing. You may want to play soothing, meditational music. Have your journal handy for the recording of any impressions.

Your Energy Pattern Exercise

Breathe through your nostrils deeply into your belly. The breath transforms into golden white light. Breathe the light into your body, watching the light penetrate deeper and deeper, down through the skin, into the tissue, into the bone, down into the very level of the cells. The light brings the healing and revivifying powers of the universal life force into the depths of your being. With every breath, you feel fresher, lighter, better. Exhale the light, sending out what is no longer needed: negativity, fatigue, waste.

As the breath restores you, become aware of a change in you. You see the breath moving through you as living energy. You yourself are a pattern of energy lines, along which beams of colored light move with incredible beauty. The lines may be straight and gridlike, or circular swirls or spirals. This is your own energy pattern, unique to you, your "fingerprint" of light.

Repeat the affirmation three times: *I am the beauty of love and light.*

Notice how responsive is your energy pattern. It reacts to every thought, every feeling. Its brightness increases and decreases. It expands and contracts. It has no finite boundaries but reaches out into infinite space, connecting you to all things in the cosmos. Allow yourself to radiate peace, love, and beauty. Notice the energy pattern and how you feel. Observe in detail what you look like as the energy of love and beauty.

Repeat the affirmation three times: *I flow in total harmony with All That Is.*

Notice how you feel being in harmony: emotions, physical sensations. Become aware of how energy flows through your body.

You can substitute another term for All That Is, such as God, the universe, the Tao, etc. Do this exercise daily until you are accustomed to seeing and sensing yourself as energy. Carry it over into your daily activities. Feel yourself flowing in whatever you do.

This exercise will help you become more centered in the body. It will focus your concentration on the moment, so that you will spend more time in the now. In the Eastern traditions, this is called mindfulness. Mindfulness teaches us to be fully present to whatever we are doing, whether it is a simple task or an important activity.

We spend a lot of time somewhere else besides the present. If you analyzed a day's worth of thoughts, you'd find that you spend most of your moments thinking about things that have already happened or anticipating things that haven't yet happened and may not.

You will be amazed at what happens to you when you spend more time in the moment. You will realize many ways you spend time unproductively and will want to change them. As you step more and more effortlessly into the flow, you will experience greater inner peace. You will feel more in harmony with everything you do. You will also realize where you are *not* in harmony. Take whatever steps you can to minimize or eliminate disharmony.

Numerous benefits come from being in the flow. Your creativity and intuition are enhanced. Your happiness and contentment rise. You feel better about yourself. All of these improve the gifts that you have to offer to your lover. The changes in your vibrations ripple out in invisible waves and affect the way others react to and interact with you. When you radiate peace and love, you receive peace and love in return. When you seek love, you must in turn be a beacon of love and harmony.

Furthermore, you develop a sense of rhythm with life, rhythm with the world, and rhythm with the cosmos. The more you feel at one with everything around you, the better you will be able to manifest your goals.

So go ahead, get in the flow, and allow the blessings to flow in return!

Connecting to Your Lover

After you have practiced becoming part of the universal flow of energies, practice meeting and merging with the energy of your destined lover. It doesn't matter if you haven't yet met him or her, or even have the slightest inkling who it is, or when and where you will meet. We will work outside the limitations of time and space. We will seek to put our energy in a harmonious flow with the energy of the universe. When we are in harmony with All That Is, we are more likely to create the reality in which we connect with the love that is meant for us.

Science has amply demonstrated the ability of our consciousness to interact with matter. In parapsychology, it is called *psychokinesis,* or "mind over matter." Psychokinesis involves such things as using thought to move objects, change environmental factors (such as the temperature of the room), and influence the behavior of something, such as the growth rate of plants. Such feats have been documented many times over in laboratory experiments. The ability of consciousness to influence matter also plays a role in areas difficult for science to measure, such as in miracles, prayer, and healing.

However, we should not think of mind *over* matter, which encourages the notion that we can force the universe to bend to our wishes. Yes, it is possible to force one's will into being, if sufficient energy is devoted to it. But anything that is forced is not natural and thus will only be problematic. It is much better to attract our good to us naturally, by having mind in harmony with matter.

This lesson of being in harmony with the flow was brought home to me one night when Tom and I attended a meeting of one of our local metaphysical groups. We arrived a bit early and joined in helping the setting up of the room. It was a warm night, and someone suggested opening the windows. Tom went over to the windows—three large, double-sashed affairs with layers of old paint on them. Now Tom is a strong, strapping fellow, but try as he might, he could not get the windows to budge. He pushed so hard on the sashes that I was afraid the glass would shatter. The windows appeared to be stuck fast, perhaps from humidity or the old paint.

As the meeting got under way, the room predictably became hotter. Suddenly a gentleman in the rear of the audience rose, went to the windows, and popped them open effortlessly, as though they were on greased sliders! Tom and I looked at each other in amazement.

After the meeting, we approached the gentleman, whose name was Chuck. We knew him from the group. He had recently given a talk on the unfoldment of his own mystical experiences.

"So, Chuck, how did you get those windows open so easily?" said Tom, explaining his own lack of success.

"It was easy," said Chuck. "When I put my hand on the windows, I could feel the vibration of the wood. I matched my vibration to it, and they came open."

Of course. A simple, everyday explanation for stuck windows!

I looked at Tom and said, "Looks like a clear case of mind over matter to me!"

"Right," said Tom. "It didn't matter what was on *my* mind—those windows weren't going to open!"

The more I thought about it, though, I saw how the situation really involved mind in harmony with matter. Chuck didn't attempt to force the windows open but rather invited the windows open through a harmony of energies. The energy of Chuck's consciousness melded with the energy of matter to yield the desired result.

I also saw how this fit in with all the mystical traditions and their concepts of thought creating reality and how the energy of visualizations, affirmations, and prayer brings results. To find our destined partner, we invite the right energies to be drawn to us through positive direction of the energies of our consciousness—our thoughts, feelings, and beliefs.

The lesson of harmony plays out in relationships. People want to know if they can *make* a relationship work. They are involved with someone they perceive as their true love, but who remains ignorant of this important fact. They have allowed themselves to become confused by projection of their desires. They are determined, through sheer force of their will, to make the universe bend—to get their square peg hammered into a round hole. It is possible to do so, but when the universe bends unnaturally, it eventually springs back, sometimes with a nasty snap.

Karin was set on making her elusive partner wake up to her as his perfect love and make a commitment. She succeeded in getting him to move in with her and then experienced nothing but trouble. There was always some upset, some emotional turmoil going on that kept Karin alternately in tears and in a rage. She finally ended the relationship. "I guess I knew deep down in my heart that it wasn't going to last in the long run," she told me, "but I ignored that and thought I could make it work, anyway."

When we are in the harmonious flow, that which is meant for us moves to us. That doesn't mean that we don't have to work for anything. We do, and quite often we have to work very hard. It does mean we do not have to apply force.

The Golden Stream Exercise

Here is one of my favorite exercises for getting into the flow. It is an excellent exercise for intuition, as well.

Imagine yourself floating down a gentle river. Notice that the water is golden. The sunlight falling upon it makes the surface sparkle like millions of golden gems. You are warm, happy, and content, floating easily down the river. You are fully present in the moment. There is no past, no tomorrow, only the eternal moment.

The gems sparkle and flash. The river of water becomes a river of light.

As you float along in the river of light, become aware of your body. It begins to change. See yourself being filled by the golden light of the sun and by the sparkles from the river. The light transforms you, turning you into a golden being. You become lighter and lighter. You see that the golden light that is now you is actually composed of millions of sparkling golden gem lights, just like the sunlight dancing on the water of the river. Allow yourself to sink deeper and deeper into this field of sparkling lights. You feel energized. Suddenly you realize that you are one and the same with the river of light.

Feel the flow of the motion of light. Allow yourself to be carried along with it. You are filled with complete peace and harmony, at one with the light.

Up ahead you see a round, golden ball of light. It is the Source of All Being, the supply of universal good. The river of light is flowing into it. A cosmic river merging into a cosmic sun. The golden sun is your desire—your union with your destined love. The river flows effortlessly into it, merging perfectly with it.

Feel yourself merging with the energy of your lover. It becomes part of you, and you become part of it. You cannot be separated from it. Stay in this space for a few moments, and notice how you feel.

When you feel ready, return to an awareness of your physical body. As you feel more solid, know that the light remains within you—the connection to all that is yours.

The next exercise further develops contact with your lover in the Eternal Now. Remember, in the seamless, undivided universe, time does not exist, and everything that is happening, has ever happened, and ever will happen, is happening *now*. In this state of being, you and your lover have already found each other!

A Walk in the Garden of Eternal Time Exercise

See yourself in a garden of great beauty and tranquillity. The colors of the trees, plants, and flowers are brilliant and intense—beyond words to describe them. A breeze riffles through the leaves, bringing refreshing scents. Birds chirp and sing. The sunlight is warm—the perfect temperature. Walk along and enjoy the atmosphere. This is the Garden of Eternal Time, where everything that is, exists. You are here to meet your soulmate.

Take a narrow dirt path that winds through the garden, past ponds and through groves of trees. There is no need to hurry, for time does not pass away. Notice the flowers, and stop to smell them. Pick a bouquet for the journey.

Up ahead, you see a stone bench by the path and a figure seated upon the bench. It is your soulmate. Your heart quickens in love and joy. Your soulmate sees you and rises to greet you. You feel the same love and joy rising in the heart of your beloved.

As you near your soulmate, you are aware of the patterns of energy of your two beings merging harmoniously together in magnificent colors. This is the soul who is meant for you, and for whom you are meant, to love and cherish and nurture. Embrace your beloved and feel the unconditional love of two hearts merging into one. It is meant to be. This love is yours. You have always had it. You have it now.

Give your beloved the flowers you picked, a gift of love and receptivity. The flower is the soul, its petals the radiance of light that is the essence of the soul. The open blossoms represent manifestation. You are manifesting your perfect love.

Exchange a message with your beloved. Give thanks to the Divine for the blessings of love. Return from the garden, knowing that you have found your soulmate *now*. Record your impressions of your soulmate, the energies, and the messages you exchanged.

The more you experience being in harmony with the flow, the more positive changes you will see in all aspects of your life. Flow exercises help to quicken the process of manifestation, not only for your soulmate, but for other goals as well. Make these exercises a part of your daily spiritual practice.

12

Prayer Power

Ask those things of God which it is worthy of God to bestow.

—SEXTUS THE PYTHAGOREAN

Prayer is an energy—a projection of our thoughts, desires, and will—directed at a unification with God or the Source of All Being, which holds the perfection of all things. When we pray for something, we are actually seeking to achieve harmony with creation so that the spiritual laws can work for us. The law of attraction is set into motion. Prayer is a powerful way of being in the flow.

As the author of four books on prayer and a committed practitioner of prayer and meditation, I am well acquainted with the power generated by heartfelt prayer. Prayer has worked for me in all areas of life. I have heard more than a thousand testimonials about the results of prayer, for everything from miraculous healing or finding love to finding jobs or finding something lost or stolen.

Nonetheless, many people say that they'd like to believe in the power of prayer, but they don't think that all prayers are answered. Nearly everyone has a story about praying for some-thing in particular, without the results they desired. People then sometimes give up on prayer. That's a shame, because the simple truth is: Prayer works, and all prayers are answered.

Every Day Is a Rainbow

Prayer helped Cindy find her soulmate after two marriages did not work.

I met someone that I noticed from a distance who really caught my eye. I knew then that everything this individual did was every-thing that I liked. I thought it was just a coincidence—how the world turns. But some time ago, I had prayed to God for a mate to love me as much as I can love them, unconditionally. If I could find that person, it would be a blessing that came from God. And so it was. We agree upon the same things. We share the same ideas. We have the same feelings in our hearts. We have the same love for God's little animals and His creations. We would rather give than receive. When one of us is weak, the other is strong, and we're able to work through situations without it getting out of hand. Even when we disagree, maybe once in awhile, it's just de-bating. It does work out between us. We get up in the mornings happy. We go to bed the same way. Our whole day is a rainbow. I never had that in the past. Prayer is a powerful thing if you be-lieve. This is someone you want to spend the rest of your earthly life with—without any reservations. God will be there for you.

The Nature of Prayer and Praying

Prayer is like quicksilver. No matter how we try to define it and contain it, its true shape eludes us. Essentially, prayer is an act of communing with God, Father/Mother/All That Is, the Divine, or the Universal Mind—pick your term depending on your spiritual or religious outlook. Prayer has existed in a multitude of forms ever since the human race became conscious and sought a connection to higher forces. Prayer is fundamental to all religions; William James once noted that prayer "is the very soul and essence of religion." Yet prayer thrives outside organized religion, too. It is the essential link that helps us bridge two worlds: our mundane world and a transcendent reality. In that transcendent world, we see all things as being possible.

Most of us define prayer as a petition to God for something specific. Or as a conversation with God. We are often taught that there are right and wrong ways to pray.

But if we take away the religious trappings, we see that prayer is simply energy. It is the energy of your thoughts, will, and intent sent out to the orchestrating matrix of the cosmos. It is first cousin to affirmations. It is also first cousin to visualization. The act of praying is a form of ritual that engages the senses and focuses intent and will.

Prayer is an attunement with the wholeness of God, the heart of God, the will of God, the All That Is. It connects us to the source of all good, which includes the love that is meant for us. When we are in harmony through attunement, we are better able to manifest what we seek.

What to pray for

Most of us want to pray for specifics, yet we sometimes feel guilty and wonder if asking for things is right. Shouldn't prayer be for a loftier purpose? Separate your heartfelt needs from your wants, and you will always feel clear about this. It's perfectly fine to pray for love, or for a better job, or whatever you need. However, you can raise the vibration of your prayer even higher if you add that you are willing to follow what is right and harmonious for you.

Pray for a love by placing it within the context of your unfoldment as a spiritual being: "Dear Creator, help me to find the right deep and loving relationship." Thus, you will raise your overall spiritual consciousness, which in turn benefits all areas of your life, including your ability to love and be loved.

The more you pray, the more you will naturally be inclined to pray for whatever is in your highest good. Specifics will fall into place, because you will be building your faith in outcomes that will be best for you.

How to pray

Daily prayer is essential. It oils the spiritual mechanisms of the universe and improves our spiritual health. Important factors are clarity—being clear about what you are praying for—and sincerity. Speak spontaneously from the heart. Compose poetic prayers for recitation. Use formal prayers that have meaning for you.

However you pray, put your heart and soul into it. Dry prayer lacks energy. The more energy you give prayer, the more prayer will work for you.

I find it helpful to engage the senses when I pray. Engaging the senses helps to bring the spiritual energy into the material plane. When possible, I light a candle and burn incense. I may play some soft, meditative music or sacred chant. I create vivid visualizations to go along with the prayer. Some of my prayer is thought and some is spoken aloud. Sometimes I sit in the silence and receive like a vessel.

I am not fond of begging prayer because it lends itself to desperation, and desperation is counterproductive to manifesting your objectives. No matter how upset or despondent I may be, I find an affirmative, positive way to frame my prayer. It always lifts my spirits.

Should we repeat a prayer? Yes, and we should repeat it often. I don't think God or the Divine Mind needs to hear anything more than once. But prayer really is more for us. Repetition builds energy and firms our focus and resolve. It helps to motivate us to take action.

Three basic answers

There is no such thing as unanswered prayer. There are three fundamental answers to all prayers:

1. "Yes." What we pray for is delivered.

2. "Not yet." We are not ready for the answer, or forces set in motion have yet to manifest in the material plane. A "not yet" answer tests our faith and patience, especially if we've been searching for a lover for a long time.

3. "Find another way." Sometimes we are fixed on answers that really aren't in our best interests ("I want *that* person"). "Find another way" directs us to look elsewhere or reexamine what we are asking for.

We are never given a flat "no" to prayer and left hanging. We are always provided guidance.

We are always pleased with "yes" answers, not so pleased with "not yet" answers, and often totally discouraged or even angry with "find another way" answers. However, many prayers are answered with "find another way." If we earnestly seek guidance through prayer, we must be prepared to accept and follow the guidance we are given. We are always given the answer that is in the highest good for each situation. What is in the highest good may be better than what we seek. Or, it may be hard, but necessary, to accept.

How Prayers Are Answered

It certainly would be easy for us if our prayers were answered by a voice booming out of the heavens. While some prayers are indeed answered by distinct and clear inner voices (and sometimes by a direct, external voice), most prayers are answered in more subtle ways. Consequently, when we are praying earnestly for something, we must keep our antennae up to catch all the signals that come our way.

All prayers are answered immediately. Sometimes it takes us awhile to recognize or accept the answer. The process of recognizing answers to prayers often is highly alchemical: it's a process of transformation that takes some time to cook in the recesses of consciousness.

Intuition

Our own intuition provides answers to prayer. We know what is right or wrong, what will work and what won't. Our bodies may provide tangible signals, such as tingling of the skin, a tightening of the stomach, and so on.

Intuition often flashes upon us in an *aha!* insight when we are least expecting it. Perhaps we get a sudden urge or idea to attend an event, take a course, or go someplace where we wind up meeting a significant other.

Synchronicity

People who pray or meditate regularly find that synchronicities dramatically increase in their lives. They achieve a certain attunement with the universe, and it speaks back to them in the form of meaningful coincidences. Mystics in the East have been aware of this phenomenon for at least 2,500 years. The Upanishads state, "When the mind rests steady and pure, then whatever you desire, those desires are fulfilled."

Synchronicities occur in words other people tell us, in meetings with strangers, in things we happen to read or hear in the media, and so on.

Dreams

Our dreams are rich sources of spiritual guidance and answers to prayers. Pray before going to bed at night. Your answers may become apparent in dreams themselves or may be clear to you upon awakening.

Keys for Successful Prayer

We can make our prayers more effective by establishing sound prayer habits. Prayer does not need to be stiff or formal; it's like having a conversation with a good friend.

Here are seven keys that will enrich your prayer life:

Key #1: Be honest.

The number-one priority in approaching prayer is to have complete honesty with yourself and God. Be honest about what you are praying for and why. With complete honesty, it becomes difficult, if not impossible, to pray for something that is selfish.

We cannot manipulate others through prayer to bend them to do what we desire. Prayer responds to the vibration of the highest good. Something that is not in the highest good will not prevail in the long run.

Barbara prayed hard for a soul commitment from Jim. Although she was convinced he was the one, she wasn't looking clearly at the relationship and its inherent weaknesses. Through sheer determination, she succeeded in establishing a live-together arrangement with a commitment—or so she thought—for marriage. It just wouldn't stick. She and Jim had karmic ties, all right, but they were not intended for a soulmate union. After months of exhausting emotional turmoil, Barbara finally let go. It took her awhile to regain her emotional equilibrium. Then she began praying the prayer she should have made in the first place: to be guided to the person who was right for her. She soon met a man who far outshone Jim in terms of the relationship he could offer Barbara.

Key #2: Make every thought a prayer.

You are what you think, goes the old adage, to which can be added, you pray as you think. Our thoughts create our reality. All our thoughts, all our conscious thinking, are in essence part of a prayer.

The great healer Ambrose Worrall observed, "For as a man thinketh, so he is. Indeed, as he thinketh, so he prays." Worrall said that we shouldn't be so concerned about how we pray but how we think.

Consequently, we should be mindful of right thinking—making every thought literally a prayer for joy, healing, love, and the good of all. We can hardly expect our prayers to be successful if we mire ourselves in negative thinking.

When you pray to meet your soulmate, be on guard for negative thoughts that crop up: "I'll never find him/her" or "No one is out there for me." These thoughts are prayers, too, that contradict your affirmative prayers.

When negative thinking occurs, gently let the thoughts go and replace them with positive ones.

Key #3: Make your life your prayer.

Similarly, we should be mindful of right living—making every act positive, loving, and constructive. The prayer that is answered is your life prayer, which is what you think and say all day long. Many people feel virtuous during prayer time, yet the rest of the time they're living contrary to their prayers. Then they wonder why their prayers do not appear to be answered. Prayer is not a substitute for action. When you petition in prayer, you must put into motion all that you can to help bring about the results you seek.

If you pray for love, then embody love. Be loving, generous, and charitable to others. What you give out will come back to you.

Making your life your prayer also means taking action on prayer. When you receive guidance, act on it.

Do your best to make your spiritual light shine. Remember, someone is out there looking for *you*.

Key #4: Pray regularly.

Set aside some time each day—even a few minutes—for prayer periods. Prayer is important in the morning, for it helps to raise spiritual consciousness and set a high tone for the day. Prayer at night is equally important to bring closure on a positive note.

Praying regularly will help you in turn make every thought, word, and deed a prayer.

Key #5: Pray in a group.

Group prayer is comforting and powerful and has a synergistic effect. That is, three people praying together, for example, will have a greater effect than three people praying separately.

The Bible encourages group prayer. In Matthew 18:20, Jesus says, "For where two or three are gathered in my name, there I am in the midst of them."

Most churches and spiritual organizations have prayer circles and services. It is not necessary to gather physically in the same spot but merely to join in collective prayer at certain specified times. Or you can ask to have names put on prayer lists, which are then prayed over by groups of people in a prayer circle.

Don't be shy about praying for love in a prayer group. The person next to you probably has the same prayer and will feel bolstered by yours.

Key #6: Have faith and patience.

Maintain confidence that your prayer will be realized in the right way and at the right time. If confidence wavers, follow the advice of minister Emmet Fox: "Stop thinking about the difficulty, whatever it is, and think about God instead." Focus on God by thinking such things as this statement of absolute Truth:

> *There is no power but God; I am the child of God, filled and surrounded by the perfect peace of God; God is love; God is guiding me now; God is with me.*

Key #7: Give thanks.

Every time you pray, remember to be thankful for all that you are blessed with in life. And give thanks for the outcome of your prayers, acknowledging that results are in concert with divine order.

*   *   *

Try these seven keys every day. You will soon notice changes in your life. You will feel calmer and more centered, and some of life's rough edges will smooth out. You will find it easier to resolve problems and to cope with stressful situations. Your relationships with others will improve as well. The path to love will open. And you will feel closer to God.

Prayers for Love

Dear Creator, Eternal Source of Good, thank you for the numberless gifts and blessings that fill my days: for life itself and its endless variety; for all that sustains body and mind; for love and friendship; for the delights of the senses; and for your presence, which deepens and enriches life. Please guide me as I seek the perfect, loving relationship meant for me. My heart is open to give and receive love. I give thanks now for this and all other blessings in my life.

Dear Creator, please help me to have patience and faith that I will find the love that is meant for me. I know that you are guiding me, and I give thanks for that guidance. I also give thanks for the love that is mine, which I draw now to my heart.

Dear Creator, thank you for the bounty of love that flows into my life. Help me to be a good partner. Help me to help both of us grow.

13

Positive Action

Suit the action to the word, the word to the action.

—SHAKESPEARE

Our thoughts, desires, wishes, intentions, affirmations, visualizations, and prayers all take on added power when we act on them physically. Action can come in the form of decisions, choices, and initiating change. Action also can come in the form of a ritual.

You might think of a ritual as something exotic, solemn, or exclusively religious. It's true that all religions and spiritual, mystical, and magical traditions have rituals for petitioning higher power and worshiping the sacred. Rituals also mark turning points in daily life. Rites of passage and initiation, weddings, funerals, and coming-of-age ceremonies are all types of ritual. Human beings have used many kinds of rituals since the dawn of our history to manifest goals: love, successful hunts, abundant harvests, good marriages, fertility, luck, prosperity, protection from harm, mystical union with God, and more.

When we engage in a ritual, we enter a space of changed and

focused consciousness. We step outside of ordinary space and time. We are in contact with a greater power that we call on for help. A ritual helps to seal our intention and set forces in motion. It creates a psychological change that bolsters our faith and belief in the outcome we are seeking and energizes us for taking the right actions.

A good ritual engages the senses in a vivid way through movement, use of the voice, sounds, scents, and even tastes. A visualization is a ritual in which we use our senses in an imaginary way to create something we desire to happen in the physical.

Rituals do not need to be formal, somber, or elaborate in order to be effective. In fact, the more enjoyable a ritual is, the more likely it will be effective for you.

Praying is a ritual, and when you add to it lighting a candle and incense, it takes on more form as a ritual. Making a wish on the full moon is a widespread and very old, simple folk ritual.

Jen placed what she called "activators" around her apartment. The activators were objects that represented what she wanted. Every night before retiring, Jen went through her apartment and touched all of the activators. The ritualistic act of repeatedly touching the objects evoked strong emotions associated with her goals, as well as vivid mental pictures. She then lit a candle and said a prayer. She went to bed every night with her faith strengthened that she would get what she envisioned. She knew she was not alone but that she was receiving divine assistance.

Altars Help You Alter Consciousness

One way to establish ritual as part of your daily spiritual practice is to create an altar in your home. Personal altars have become increasingly popular. People use them to create sacred
space at home and for rituals of all kinds.

Small accent tables and boxes make excellent altars and can
be set up in a corner of your bedroom or other area of the
house that does not get a lot of general traffic. If you do not have
space for a permanent altar, you can keep your altar objects in a
special box and get them out whenever you wish to do a ritual.
I keep a portable altar in a fabric jewelry roll. It's ready to go
whenever I need to travel, and it can be set up anywhere.

For your soulmate altar, you will want to have on hand both
basic and personal objects. The basics are:

- A cloth to cover the altar top. If your space is small, this
  might be a pretty cloth napkin or handkerchief.

- Representatives of the four elements. A candle serves for
  fire; incense or a feather serve for air; a stone, crystal, or
  dish of salt serve for earth; a shell or a small dish of water
  serve for water. Having symbols of the four elements
  represents being in balance with the natural world.

- Devotional objects. These include religious objects, images, statues, and symbols, as well as objects of personal
  significance that foster your connection to the Divine.
  Devotional objects symbolize connection to the spiritual realms.

In addition to these basics, you can add any objects that assist you with your purpose. For finding a soulmate, such objects might be a picture of a happy couple, a photo of a favorite romantic place, a ring, and so on.

Having an altar space at home will help you keep your intent focused and energized. It also will aid your spiritual practice in general, serving as the meeting place with guides and God.

A Tangible Thought Altar

Sheryl was a divorced mom whose fiancé had died. Even after a long time had passed, Sheryl still mourned him, but she knew she had to get on with her life. She attended a seminar on visualization, intrigued by the idea that you create your own reality by setting your intention. At the seminar, she learned how to create a tantha altar to use as a tool in visualization. *Tantha* stood for "tangible thought." Praying and visualizing at the tantha altar was a ritual to set intention and create a new reality.

Sheryl left the seminar feeling energized and empowered. While she was driving home, a strong thought suddenly popped into her mind: *I'm going to meet my husband at the ———Inn.* The thought was so urgent that she couldn't disregard it. It seemed like something that came from a higher part of herself, her Higher Self.

She changed course and drove straight to the inn instead of going home. She went into the bar, ordered a drink, and sat down with pen and paper. She listed all the qualities and characteristics that she wanted in her ideal partner, allowing them to flow swiftly from the center of her heart.

When the list was finished, there were thirty-five specific traits. Her ideal man was there on paper, but where was he in person? No one stepped forward. What about the intense inner conviction that she was going to meet her future husband here?

Despite the fact that no man materialized, Sheryl did not feel let down. She still had the feeling that she would soon meet this man, and that her being at the inn that night was somehow important to this happening.

Sheryl folded up the list and went home, where she set to work to create the tantha altar she had learned about in the seminar. The altar would help focus Sheryl's intention to find her ideal mate through visualization and as much vivid sensory stimuli as possible.

The altar was a simple affair: a cardboard box covered with pretty silk scarves. On it Sheryl placed objects—the tangible things—representing the qualities she'd listed. She didn't include objects for all thirty-five traits, which would have cluttered the altar, but she chose ones that seemed to have the most energy. For example, she wanted someone with whom she could share intellectual conversations. This was represented by a book of poetry. A laughing Buddha represented being witty and having a good sense of humor. Several rocks represented a love of the earth and outdoors, hiking, gardening, and farming. Sheryl also placed on the altar a votive candle and incense burner.

Every morning before she went to work, Sheryl lit her candle and some incense and focused vivid and intense thoughts and feelings about meeting the man who would embody all the things she desired. This created a ritual in which she sent out a call and a prayer into the universe for divine help.

One week later, Sheryl's mother persuaded her to attend a

dance sponsored by Parents Without Partners. Sheryl did not want to go, but her mother convinced her that it would help her get over her grieving. Reluctantly she agreed. Shortly after they arrived, a nice-looking man asked Sheryl to dance. She turned him down curtly. Upset, she bummed a cigarette from her mother—despite the fact that she had quit smoking a year earlier—and went outside.

While she smoked, she looked up at the moon and started talking to it. She felt badly that she had snapped at the man who had asked her to dance. He had seemed very sweet and sincere, and she had just rudely pushed him away. This was no way to meet a good date, let alone a prospective husband. "Please help me get rid of this bad attitude," she begged the moon.

Back inside, Sheryl saw the man she'd rejected. He was standing on the opposite side of the room. Steeling her courage, she walked up to him, smiled, and said, "You know, I think I'm ready to dance now."

As Sheryl was to quickly discover, the man matched all thirty-five of her wish list traits. They were soon married.

There was only one point on which Sheryl had not been specific, and which turned out differently than she'd expected. She expected that her ideal man would be from the Southwest, an area of the country she loved and longed to return to. But Tom was from the local city—the southwestern part of it, that is.

As for the role of her unexpected trip to the inn, Sheryl was convinced that it was crucial to setting forces in motion. "I do feel that I first 'met' Tom at the inn," said Sheryl. "That's where the vision was created, and I could feel with certainty that it would really happen."

A Well-Oiled Prayer

In the next story, a young woman employed the principles of ritual with prayer and the making of a special oil. Oils made according to specific recipes and procedures have long been used in rituals. In Christianity, for example, holy oil is created by special blessing from a priest and is used in anointing and by the faithful for healing. The oil itself has no mystical and or magical power but serves as a powerful symbol of a personal relationship with the Divine. The act of using the oil helps to awaken within the user a partnership of power between the user and the Divine. Belief and faith on the part of the user are very important to the process.

Amanda set her intention to find her soulmate and prayed for the right person to come along. Interestingly, her parents seemed to enjoy a soulmate relationship. Her mother had always told her that she met Amanda's father after praying that God would send her husband to her. They were married in less than six months of first meeting one another, and more than twenty-five years later were still happily married. Here is Amanda's story.

James and I met at college through mutual friends. My roommate was an acquaintance of his, and he had stopped to talk to the two of us one day in the fall. I remember the first time I met him, but I didn't think much of it at the time. I was interested in another guy, and James had a girlfriend from his old school in another state. He doesn't remember meeting me at all that time; for several months, he thought my name was Sarah, when it's really Amanda.

That spring, James's girlfriend broke up with him, and my interest in this other relationship had come to nothing. He was stunned by his breakup. I was devastated by the rejection I had faced from this other guy. I spent most of the summer depressed about it and was generally dreary about finding anyone at all to be with for my last year at college. I had overwhelming fears that I would never find anyone and would spend the rest of my life alone. I realize now that was very melodramatic, but it was how I felt at the time.

I decided the best thing for me to do would be to let go of this failed attempt at a relationship. In the past, I would have just prayed about it, but this time I used a method rather different than anything before. I was raised my whole life to be a very conservative Christian, the religion of my parents and most of my extended family. But on my own I had been studying Wicca. I have not embraced that as my own religion, but there are aspects of it that have drawn me into a greater understanding of my own faith.

In August I wrote out a prayer to God for finding my soulmate—the one person best meant for me, whom I could spend the rest of my life with. It was what I desired more than anything else. I also prepared an oil from some of the methods I had researched from Wiccan practices.

Please let me make clear that I was not in any way intending to cast a spell, or anything like that. This was simply as a reminder to myself that I had prayed specifically for this thing, to find a relationship that would be healthy to me, and make me realize that I am taken care of in this world. There is an account in the Old Testament of Jacob anointing a rock as an act of worship to show God's protection of him, and this was the sort of thing that I had in mind when I was making the oil.

Around this same time, James and I became better and better friends. I went to visit my roommate, who was spending the summer on campus, as was James. The three of us, as well as some others, went on a picnic together, and we would often get together to play board games, watch movies, and hang out. James was over at our place almost every night, but I didn't think much of it. He had the most impossible roommates on campus, and everyone pitied him. Plus, we fed him, and like a stray, he kept coming around at dinnertime. (He later told me that he had a crush on me from the first time we went on a picnic together with our friends, but I was blind to it, not thinking that he was my type.)

At the beginning of September, I moved back to school, and my regular routine began again. I would have forgotten all about the prayer I had made nearly a month before if the jar of oil I had made hadn't been sitting next to my cosmetics and perfume bottles, just waiting.

I can distinctly remember the night that I remembered the bottle of oil. It was a Monday in late September. A petty argument with one of my housemates had upset me very much, and in my dark mood, I felt that God had abandoned me and forgotten my prayer. A whole month had passed since school began, and I hadn't been asked out by a single guy! I took the bottle of oil and a flashlight and went for a walk.

The campus was deep in the countryside, surrounded by woods alternating with farmland. I stuck to the woods and walked for what seemed like forever. It was dark. I pretended that I wasn't afraid, though in truth, I am easily scared of the dark. I had a specific place in mind, but I couldn't find it in the dark. I came to another clearing, and deciding that it did not matter, I stopped there. I dumped the bottle of oil out. I hadn't noticed at first, be-

cause I had stepped just a little way off the path where it was over-
grown, but I had just dumped the bottle of oil out onto a rock. I
thought it very ironic at the time. I marched back home, still furi-
ous, hurt, and confused.

James was there when I got back. He had brought us food, for
a change. It was his birthday that day, and some of the ladies
where he worked had baked him a cake, and he had brought what
was left over to us. I hadn't been home hardly any time at all before he asked me to go on a walk with him. I went, more to humor
him for his birthday than anything, but we had a wonderful time.
We got to talking seriously, as we had never done before. I'm a
very private person, often described as "hard to get to know" and
do not like talking over serious things very easily.

At one point, we stopped to sit and watch the stars. He saw a
shooting star, which I told him was lucky, since it was his birthday.
I know he made a wish, because much later, he told me what it
was—to go out with me. By the time I got back home, I realized
that I liked him a lot. He was so easy to talk to, it seemed almost
natural to tell him about anything.

Every night that week he asked me to go out for a walk with
him in the evenings. We walked for what seemed like hours and
talked about everything. By Friday night, he kissed me and asked
me for our first real date. I agreed.

We had a romantic dinner at an Italian restaurant, but the
coolest part of the evening happened while we were in line at the
concession stand of the theater. We were going to get popcorn and
pop, and he told me, in the most serious tones, that I could do
whatever I wanted, but he had a strict rule: He never ate the popcorn before the movie started. I laughed at him and asked him
which of my friends had told him. He was very confused, asking

what they were supposed to have told him. I assumed that someone, maybe my roommate, had told him my habit of never eating popcorn until the movie starts. They often teased me about it, but it was something I have done for as long as I can remember. Even my family knows about it, because I've always been that way, even though none of them do it. But it turns out, no one told him. He was serious; he had the same habit as me!

As we got to know each other better, it turned out that we had an almost unbelievable amount of things in common. Our passions and interests are very similar. I am a writer, with a dream to write full time, and he is studying for his master's to become a professor. We love used bookstores, and had many of our first dates browsing through various used bookstores, drifting together and separately through the overcrowded stacks. We have remarkably similar outlooks and beliefs. We spent one night talking in a coffeehouse for four hours, mostly about God and various fine details of religion.

We had been dating for a week when I knew I loved him. I'm not usually so forward in that kind of thing, with all the awkwardness that is usually involved in a new relationship. But I felt so safe and comfortable around him, that it just sort of slipped out. And he told me he loved me, too. It wasn't strange or awkward at all. It felt normal, as if everything were as it should be. I feel safer with him than I ever have in my whole life.

Eight months after we started dating, he asked me to marry him. Some people told us that they thought it was too soon, but the people who knew us best joked that we couldn't be married soon enough. I don't have any doubts or reservations at all. I know it is absolutely perfect. We both talk, dream, making plans for our future, talking about things five, ten, twenty, or forty years down the road—what it will be like to have children, where we might be when we are old together.

Once I invited my old roommate (my maid of honor) to go with James and me to an event we were attending. She laughed, wanting to know if I shouldn't first ask James if it were all right if she tagged along. It hadn't even occurred to me, because I knew he would be fine with it, happy to have her along. She was laughing because she had gotten an E-mail from him earlier that same day, which I hadn't known anything about, in which he had invited her to this exact same event. He hadn't asked me, either; he just knew that it was something that I would want. We often startle people with our similarity in thought— it is almost like mind reading.

We were separated for a time, and so we used the Internet to chat in the evenings. I couldn't count the number of times I would be looking away from the screen, typing a question to him, only to look up, and see he had just asked, phrased just slightly different, the same exact question. We joke about being telepathic, but at times it seems almost like he can read my mind. He is better at telling my feelings than anyone I've ever known, and to a lesser extent, I can do the same with him. He was the first one to call us soulmates, but as soon as he said it, I knew it was true.

In your inner work, you will be inspired with ways to put your own vision into action. Follow the guidance, and trust the process!

14

Dream Power

I arise from dreams of thee
In the first sweet sleep of night
When the winds are breathing low,
And the stars are shining bright.

— PERCY BYSSHE SHELLEY

The search for a soulmate goes on even when we sleep. Through dreams, we are given information and guidance and perhaps even a sneak preview of what is to come. In sleep, our busy mind is at rest, and intuition, spiritual helpers, and the voice of God can speak.

Perhaps you've always thought of dreams as nonsensical jumbles of strange images and incomplete stories. But if you've kept a dream journal and worked with your dreams, you know what human beings around the world have known since ancient times: that our dreams deliver truth and have great power to transform and heal.

The ancient view of dreams is that they are literally a bridge to God or the gods. In the mysterious dreamworld, human consciousness can be contacted by presences beyond, from heaven and even the realm of the dead. Dream interpretation has at times been an esteemed profession. Today, psychotherapists serve as the modern dream interpreters. Actually, *facilitator* is a more appropriate term, for we hold dreams to be unique to the dreamer, who makes the sole determination of what they ultimately mean. Dreamwork facilitators can help individuals discover the meaning of their dreams. I have worked as a lay dreamwork facilitator for more than a decade. Dreamwork is continually exciting and has much to teach us about the general nature of consciousness, as well as what goes on within the individual.

Dreams speak in symbols, a language far better than words at conveying understanding. Words are heard or seen in an intellectual way. Symbols are felt and experienced in an intuitive way. I recommend dreamwork as a part of spiritual work, for all purposes.

In our efforts to meet our soulmate, we can put dream power to work for us. To do so, we make use of an ancient practice: dream incubation. Humanity learned thousands of years ago that dreams do not have to be random. We can specifically direct and manage them to help us and accomplish our objectives.

In the classical world, dream incubation was especially used for healing. The sick and afflicted would make pilgrimages to one of hundreds of dream temples, where they would undergo rituals of purification and then petition the god of healing, Aesculapius, for help. They then went to sleep in a special dormitory. In answer, the god or one of his familiars would visit the dreamer and heal him in his dream or else provide information on how healing could be accomplished. Dream priests facilitated this process and interpreted the dreams.

Getting Dream Guidance About Soulmates

In dream incubation today, we can, in the temple of our own home, ask our dreams specific questions about soulmates.

The process is simple. Set aside a night when you will be able to relax before retiring. Go easy on food, stimulants, and alcohol, especially close to the time you retire, for these may disrupt the sleep cycle. Think of a question. Some examples are:

"Where will I meet my soulmate?"

"Who is my soulmate?"

"How can I find my soulmate?"

"Will I find my soulmate in/at————?"

Concentrate on the question throughout the day. Writing it down also helps to set it in your consciousness.

Prior to going to sleep, meditate on the question. Give yourself an affirmation that you will receive the information you need in your dreams and that you will remember them upon awakening. Give thanks for the help.

As soon as you awaken, write down whatever you can remember, even if only fragments. When you have the time, work with the dream to unlock its message. Sometimes the message will be obvious to you; other times you will need to use your intuition. A good dream book can help you work with the symbols.

Pay attention as well to the thoughts you have upon awakening. The intuition is often crisp and clear at this time. In my experience with incubation, I sometimes do not remember dream images but have a clarity of consciousness on the matter as I awaken.

Sometimes the answer does not come immediately. It's not unusual to have to repeat an incubation several times, especially if you are new at working with your dreams.

Using Dreams to Meet a Soulmate

Author Russ Michael began dreaming of his soulmate about two years before they met. The dreams arose spontaneously, not as the result of incubation. In them, he found himself in the company of the same beautiful, alluring woman. There was a vague and mysterious familiarity to her. At first, Michael thought he was dreaming of a previous love, but then he realized the dream woman was someone entirely different.

> Some of these soulmate dreams were ordinary enough, except that after each one I always felt wonderfully uplifted when I awoke. At other times, our courtship in dreams was exquisite. The dreams were romantic, passionate, and like no other dreams I could remember! In the morning, I would awaken with such greatly enhanced zest and vitality that the feeling would last through the entire day. There were times when the warm soothing aura of my ecstatic dream encounters would physically permeate and linger in my conscious mind for days afterwards.

One day, Michael was inspired to try incubating one of these dreams. Before going to sleep, he stated an affirmation: "Tonight,

I am going to dream about my dream girl again." Nothing happened for three nights, but on the fourth night, he found himself "plunged into a long and vivid dream romance" with the mystery woman. After that, he was able to incubate dreams with her several nights a week.

Incubating the dreams apparently aided the manifestation process, for about six months later, Michael and the dream woman, Pam, met. When he told her about his dreams, she was astonished; she had had similar dreams of him as a mystery lover.

Try this type of incubation yourself. Instead of asking a question about how, when, or where, make an affirmation that you will meet your soulmate in your dreams. You may have an experience similar to Michael's, or it may be similar to this one from a man named Clive.

I met my soulmate in a dream. I don't remember details about her appearance, but in the dream there was an intensity of the purest love I have ever felt. It seemed like we were out in space somewhere. It was so vivid, it didn't seem like a dream.

Soulmate dreams often are a type of dream that is more a literal experience than a symbolic one. The dream is real in that it has its own reality, just as does waking consciousness. These are *encounter dreams,* because they often involve an encounter with a person or being seemingly from another dimension or plane of existence. Encounter dreams often are characterized by intense emotions, colors, atmosphere, and a sense of it being real, not a dream.

Dream Visualizations

As we leave waking consciousness and descend into sleep, we pass through a border state of consciousness called the *hypnagogic state*. This stage of sleep is often characterized by flitting images and sounds of voices. We may still be aware of our physical environment.

Robert Monroe, who explored the frontiers of out-of-body travel, called this state "mind awake body asleep." It was in this twilight phase that he was able to journey out of his body.

The borderland of sleep creates a unique arena for conscious penetration of other realities. The dreaming mind is opening the door to expanded awareness, and the rational mind can still function. A visualization as we enter sleep can influence how we dream.

Erik, a veteran explorer of dreams and consciousness, uses a visualization of a gateway to program dreams.

As I fall asleep, I hold in my mind the image of a gateway. It's an image that came to me in meditation, and I have built it up over time with detail. It's high and arched and carved out of glowing white and gold stone. It looks like the entrance to an ancient, sacred temple. The gateway symbolizes the way to something I want to explore in dreaming consciousness. I alter the visualization, depending on what it is that I want to experience.

You can create a visualization to meet your soulmate. Images such as a doorway, gateway, or portal are important, for these symbolize passage into a different reality. In meditation, allow an image to rise spontaneously in the mind. Then, as you prepare for sleep, see the gateway. As you pass through it, affirm, "I am going to meet my soulmate," or another statement that feels appropriate.

As a variation, see the gateway as the entrance to the Akashic Records or Hall of Records, said to be the repository of everything that has ever happened, is happening, and will happen. There in the hall, you will look up information on your soulmate.

"I believe I literally dreamed my soulmate into my life," a woman named Kate told me. She described her experience.

I believe in the power of dreams, and I have recorded mine for years. I've had a lot of amazing dreams that I can honestly say have changed my life. Five years ago, my marriage ended when my husband left me for someone else. I was devastated, because I was convinced that we were destined to be together. How could he possibly leave me? As I healed myself, I came to see that I had projected an expectation onto the relationship that hadn't been there.

I was determined not to repeat the mistake and also not to settle for less the next time around. I wanted to find the person I was truly destined to be with—my soulmate. I knew my dreams could help me.

In meditation, I asked for the right visualization for this purpose. The image that came to me was of me riding a bus. The bus went out and out into the countryside. Finally, it stopped, and the driver indicated that I had to get out. I was alone. In front of me was a bridge. The road on the other side disappeared into the distance. Way, way far away, I could see a figure walking down the road. Somehow I knew this was my soulmate, and that we would meet in actuality when one of us crossed the bridge or we met in the middle.

When I went to sleep, I would call up this visualization. For some reason, I was never able to cross the bridge myself. I had the understanding that it was my soulmate who needed to make the journey over. So, every night, I would enter this image and mentally call out to him that I was waiting for him on the other side of the bridge. I would hold this picture as I fell asleep. The progress was slower than what I wanted, but I could never seem to get him to hurry up. He moved along at his own pace.

One night I had a very vivid dream in which I found myself standing by the bridge in my visualization. This time, my soulmate was at the foot of the other end. He crossed over and reached out his hand, and I reached out mine. When we touched, I felt an electric shock that was so strong, it woke me up.

I knew, with a deep conviction, that this dream signaled that my soulmate was about to come into physical reality. And in fact, that's what happened, not long after that.

Once Ben and I were talking about how fabulous it was that we came together. He said, "I had to come a long way to find you," referring to all the changes he'd gone through prior to meting me. "I guess somehow I knew you were out there—my radar was picking up your signals." A weird feeling went through me when he said that, because at that point I hadn't told him about the dreams.

I'm sure we would have found each other somehow, but I do think my active dreams had a lot to do with it!

Bridges, like gateways, are a symbol of passage to a different reality. The bridge in Kate's experience may also have symbolized Ben's process of bridging changes that were necessary for him and Kate to meet.

Lucid Dream Experiences

Some dreamers experience lucidity, or knowing they are dreaming while they are dreaming. Like encounter dreams, lucid dreams often have unusual colors, feelings, and other distinguishing characteristics that set them apart from ordinary dreams. Most of us have lucid dreams at least occasionally; some people have them frequently, and many can incubate or program them at will. One of the outstanding hallmarks of lucidity is the ability to manage the dream. The dreamer feels great elation and a sense of power.

If you find yourself lucid in a dream, ask to meet your soulmate. He or she may immediately be present, and you can then have a realistic interaction. You may be able to direct the dream as you please.

You can incubate lucid dreams through affirmation as you fall asleep: "I will know I am dreaming while I dream, and I will remember my dreams." Like any other incubation, you may have to try it repeatedly before you have success.

Sending Messages to Soulmates in Dreams

Our dreams also serve as an efficient telegraph system. We can use them to communicate with others, including the soulmate whom we have yet to meet. I know this works, for I have transmitted messages and images to others via the dreaming mind.

Compose a message. Keep it short, for long messages will disintegrate as you fall asleep. For example: "This is Susan in Smalltown. I'm waiting for you. Let's meet." You can experiment with a time frame: "This is Susan in Smalltown. I'm waiting for you. Let's meet within three months."

Repeat the affirmation as you go into sleep. Upon awakening, record whatever you remember of your dreams, as well as your waking intuitions and insights.

Using Dreams for Partnership Growth

Once you have connected with your soulmate, do not stop dreamwork. Your dreams can be an ongoing source of insight that helps the relationship develop and grow. In incubation, you can ask how to help each other, how to increase love, and how to benefit your family. You can ask for the spiritual purpose of your relationship to be revealed and for past lives to be shown. When you must make major decisions, both of you can incubate dreams for guidance. You can ask for the future to be shown to you.

Here is a testimony from a woman named Dana.

Bill and I love to discuss our dreams. We find that often, even without conscious intention, we dream similar dreams on the same night. Our dreams provide us an incredibly rich source of inspiration and guidance. Dreamwork is a different way of connecting with each other—it's like exploring each other's interior. It definitely has increased our bond and intimacy. We've had so many insights as a result of our dreams.

Having the same or a similar dream on the same night is called *mutual dreaming,* another phenomenon of the dream-world. People who share a close emotional bond can be surprised by the extent of their mutual dreaming, but of course, you have to talk about your dreams in order to make that discovery. I believe that mutual dreaming is more widespread than we might think, and that we also share some dreams with our broader circle of family and friends.

Ultimately, our dreams allow us to experience the Great Mystery behind all things. Dreams are unbounded; in them eternity and infinity spread before us.

15

Feng Shui and Your Love Chi

A place for everything and everything in its place.

—ISABELLA MARY BEETON

Feng shui is an ancient Chinese art of using the natural energies of the universe to your maximum advantage. Chi, the Chinese term for the universal life force, constantly flows everywhere, even through solid objects. A good flow of chi stimulates well-being, health, prosperity, and happiness. A poor flow of chi contributes to stagnation and negativity. Natural features of the landscape, such as mountains and rivers, affect the flow of chi in any given location. Man-made features, such as buildings, also affect chi. The art of feng shui (pronounced *fong schway*) involves sensing the flow of chi and creating factors that enhance it.

Feng shui has been around for about 4,000 years, and it has been used to plan and design both home and work spaces in the East. However, few people in the West had heard of feng shui as recently as two decades ago. Today, feng shui is a popular tool in the design of homes and office spaces in the West as well as the East. Feng shui can influence every aspect of life, including romance, sexual happiness, and family harmony. If you wish to improve your love life, feng shui can be a valuable tool.

Years of study are required to become an expert in feng shui. However, we can use a few simple basics to make substantial changes in our environment.

How Feng Shui Works

The term *feng shui* means "wind and water," two of the principal means by which chi is carried throughout the environment. Chi also is distributed by light, sound, and solar energy. Natural and man-made features can speed chi up and slow it down. When chi is fast-moving, it is very active and stimulating. It is yang chi, or masculine. When chi is slow-moving, it is peaceful and calm. This kind of chi is yin, or feminine. Too much yang chi is stressful, and too much yin chi is stagnating. Too much yang flies around and out without becoming anchored. Too much yin collects in pools and fails to energize. The ideal is to have the right mix of energies to accomplish your goals.

Feng shui is oriented according to a compass of eight directions. Each direction governs an aspect of life, similar to the way each house of an astrological horoscope governs certain activities. The southeast governs long-term relationships, engagements, and marriage. The southwest governs family and domestic harmony.

When a feng shui expert assesses a home, he looks at the flow of chi in the natural landscape and whether or not the home is ideally situated to benefit from the chi. Chi can be directed by placement of objects. The expert also examines each room in a house and determines how the things in it can be placed for maximum chi effect. Colors, shapes, and materials influence chi. Plants, mirrors, tabletop fountains, candles, and small chimes also are useful in directing energy flows. If changes in relationships and domestic harmony are desired, the expert pays special attention to the southeast and southwest corners of every room.

Enhancing the Love and Romance Corners

Here are some general guidelines to keep in mind for improving your love chi.

Colors

Bright and warm colors, such as reds and oranges, speed up chi, while pastel and cool colors, such as greens and blues, slow chi down. Yellow is a mediating color and can influence chi either way, depending upon other color combinations. If your love life has been slow to nonexistent, try adding a dash of warm colors to your southeast corners. If you have little difficulty finding relationships but can't seem to make them last, your chi may need to slow down. Try cooler colors. You needn't replace your furniture or window treatments; you can alter the color energy with accent pillows, wall hangings and art, accent rugs, and even small decorative items that can be set on tabletops.

Shapes

Sharp edges and corners and pointed shapes are yang, while soft contours and rounded shapes are yin. Experiment with furniture and pillows and plants with spiky leaves or rounded leaves to increase or decrease chi.

Materials

What are your furniture, accessories, and decorations made of? Glass, marble, faux marble, metal, and other hard, shiny, and reflective materials will speed up chi. Fabric and wood slow chi down. You can move accent pieces to more strategic locations or add inexpensive decorations to alter chi.

Chi in the Bedroom

All rooms in a home should benefit relationships, but the room that needs the most attention is, of course, the bedroom. Many people prefer a northern location for their master bedroom, for the chi in this location enhances relaxation and peaceful sleep. A bedroom on the western side of the home, however, stimulates romance. If you do not have a western bedroom and cannot relocate your bedroom to that side of your home, you can still improve the romantic ambience by paying attention to the western side of your existing bedroom.

Besides romance and a pleasing sex life, your bedroom is the place where you regenerate yourself. Because of the amount of time you spend there, special considerations should be made when taking into account the level of chi activity. Even if you need to speed up your love chi to anchor soulmate energy, you still need your bedroom to be soft and relaxing—a yin place rather than a yang place.

General ambience

Choose plants that have rounded leaves rather than spiky leaves, and wood furniture that has soft contours. Use soft lighting. Candles are soft but enhance romantic fire and passion. Select bed linens made of all-natural fibers such as cotton, linen, or silk. Soft window treatments, such as scalloped valances and drapes with shirring or soft folds, are beneficial. Wall-to-wall carpeting is preferable to area rugs. If you cannot install wall-to-wall carpeting, cover as much of the floor as possible. Remember that warm colors will increase chi, and cool colors will decrease it. Make judicious use of stimulating colors. If you overdo them, you will defeat your purpose.

Bed

A wood frame for your bed is better than a metal frame. Waterbeds seem romantic, but they are not advisable, as they create a damp environment that in turn dampens chi.

Keep the space beneath the bed clear, even if you have a dust ruffle that hides the space. Clutter under the bed clutters sleep and romance.

The direction in which the head of the bed points also influences chi. West enhances romance, contentment, income, and sleep. Southeast encourages good communication, creativity, and activity. Southwest encourages peaceful relationships, and is beneficial more for relationships that are well-established. East stimulates growth and new things.

Avoid having the head face north, which, though tranquil, may be too yin for attracting new love. Northeast and south also are not desirable for love chi. Both are disquieting to sleep, and a southern direction may also increase the risk of argumenta- tiveness in a relationship. A northwest direction is best for par- ents, as it enhances authority and control.

Depending on your room, you may have to place a bed kitty- cornered in order to obtain the desired direction. If the bedhead does not rest against a wall—which slows chi in a positive way—then use a headboard.

Mirrors

Mirrors in the bedroom are not good chi. Mirrors reflect your own chi back to you during sleep, making it more difficult to let go of old emotions and old business. Especially do not have mirrors at the foot of your bed. If you wish to keep mir- rors in the bedroom, you can turn or cover them at night.

Many modern homes have built-in mirrors on the insides of doors and the sliding doors of closets. It may not be feasible to eliminate them, but you can minimize their effect on chi by po- sitioning the bed so that you do not look into your reflection.

Pairing objects

Pairs of objects reinforce relationship energy. Objects that make pleasing pairs are candles, lamps, vases, keys, matching pic- ture frames, figurines, and so on.

Photographs

Do not keep photographs of others in your bedroom, espe- cially if you are trying to attract a soulmate. The bedroom is for romantic partnerships. Photos of family members and pets belong in other rooms. Photographs of yourself are fine. Once you are in your relationship, place in the bedroom a photo of the two of you together. This will reinforce romance and partnership chi.

Romance enhancers

A gentle but effective stimulation to romantic chi is to place something red or purple in relationship corners of the bedroom: for example, red flowers or a purple candle. Use a metal pot or holder, which enhances the overall western energy of the room.

Be creative, too, and make the bedroom uniquely yours. Things that please you will likely please your partner.

Anne's Story

Anne was grieving the death of her lover. When she felt ready to enter a relationship again, she started dating. There were disappointments and successes, but nothing really clicked. Nonetheless, the experiences helped her regain her confidence. When a long-distance relationship sagged, Anne resolved to set a very clear intent about finding her ideal partner. She announced to the universe, "I'm tired of long-distance dating, and I want more intellectual stimulation. I'm making it loud and clear that I'm ready for what I really want."

Anne did not draw up a list, but she had definite ideas about what she wanted. She created vivid and emotionally intense visualizations. She consulted a feng shui expert and reenergized her home. Anne placed objects in all the relationship corners that had strong emotional meaning to her regarding what she desired in a relationship. Thus, every time she looked at them, she gave herself a strong, positive reinforcement about her ideal relationship.

In the relationship corner of her bedroom, Anne placed a pair of white candles and a book on kisses. These symbolized to her a perfect match in the highest good, and satisfying emotional and physical intimacy. She also added a picture of red flowers in full bloom and a photo of a couple dancing. Since the couple was anonymous, the photo did not contradict the feng shui of the room. It served as a symbol of Anne's desire.

In the relationship corner of her dining room, Anne placed a pair of antique plates with fluted edges that fit perfectly together, and she filled them with diamondlike crystals. In her living room relationship corner, she placed an animated toy, which represented fun and playfulness.

Anne visualized herself dancing and enjoying herself with a partner. Out in public, she studied couples. Once it was difficult for her to look at couples without envy, but now she paid special attention to the positive things she noticed about them. She felt this got her out of her "Poor Me I'm All Alone" syndrome and raised her consciousness to a higher, more optimistic level.

A week later, Anne took her dog for a walk in the park. She was running late and was dressed in baggy, nondescript clothing, certainly not the kind of outfit intended to catch the attention of a potential partner. Entering the park at the same time was a man who caught her eye and smiled. She noticed the dog paw prints on his T-shirt, and then the University of Connecticut logo—the state where Anne was born. They struck up a conversation and soon discovered that they shared many mutual interests and habits. Anne is now happily dancing through life with the partner she manifested.

Intuitive Feng Shui

Feng shui is first cousin to the metaphysical practices of positive thinking, affirmation, visualization, and prayer. You can use the principles of environmental feng shui to bring your mental and spiritual practice into your physical environment. Feng shui can help to make your visualizations a reality. Sometimes you may practice feng shui intuitively, without knowing so or why.

Ed enjoyed home-cooked meals. In his family, the center of family life was the kitchen. Shared meals were part of the heartbeat of family. But Ed wasn't much of a cook himself. In fact, as a single man, his cooking repertoire consisted almost entirely of microwaved dinners. One of the things he wanted most in a soulmate relationship was sharing cozy, intimate meals at home. He wasn't looking for a gourmet chef, but he envisioned a relationship where he and his love would cook anything from simple to elaborate meals and enjoy each other's company.

Ed had a strong vision of this scenario. There would be relaxed evenings and candlelit dinners that would be part of the deep sharing he desired in a partner. Ed poured a great deal of emotional energy and intensity into this scenario, and into other "scenes of the perfect life," as he called them.

One day Ed experienced a strong urge to acquire things that, as a bachelor, he felt he didn't need: dinnerware, cooking utensils, glasses, and so on. He had the bare necessities and had thought that the rest would sort itself out after he was in the right relationship. But the urge wouldn't go away. He felt he had to have certain things *now*. Ed did his best to ignore it. Why get anything he wouldn't use?

One day Ed had to go to a department store. It was a big sale day, and placards touted the huge savings to be had in the home department. Normally he would have paid no attention to them, but now they seemed like irresistible beacons. He bought some inexpensive cooking pots and baking pans and stored them away in his kitchen. Soon thereafter, his neighborhood community hosted a yard sale, and he picked up an eclectic, mismatched assortment of inexpensive china and glassware. These items also went into his cupboard. Ed continued his microwave meal lifestyle.

But the acquisition of the tangible items and their placement in their true and proper location, the kitchen, subtly altered the feng shui of Ed's intention. Now in his visualizations he could see himself and his soulmate using the things he'd bought as part of their romantic evenings at home. Thus the thought of one of the things he desired in a relationship became more anchored in physical reality.

Three months later, Ed met a woman whom he felt was the one. He knew it in every cell of his being. Madeleine seemed like she had stepped straight out of his "scenes of the perfect life."

Maddy enjoyed entertaining at home. She loved to have friends over. She was a great cook and set beautiful tables. Early in the relationship, Ed was living his dream. As for mealtime, they enjoyed sharing in the cozy evenings he'd envisioned. He would help Maddy with the food preparation, and she would help him with the cleanup.

In the beginning, the relationship centered around Maddy's condo but then began shifting more and more to Ed's townhouse. The first time Maddy said she would come over to Ed's and fix dinner there, he protested. "I haven't got all the things you've got," he said. "You know how I've lived. It's been pretty bare bones."

"Surely you've got pots and plates and glasses," said Maddy. "Who needs anything more?"

"Well, it won't be like your place," he said somewhat apologetically.

When Maddy inspected his cupboards, she wasn't at all dismayed. "This is great!" she exclaimed as she looked at the mismatched pieces. "You have a real eye for putting things together."

Maddy loved Ed's eclectic kitchen collection. What had seemed happenstance to him looked to her like an artfully assembled look. They began hosting small dinner parties at Ed's, during which Maddy would extol the beauty of Ed's eclectic eye. The two of them loved to browse the flea markets and antique malls looking for pieces to add to their unique collection.

By following his natural intuition, Ed created a feng shui that enhanced his environmental chi and reinforced his mental, emotional, and spiritual chi. "I didn't know anything about feng shui at the time," Ed said. "Now I understand its principles, and I make more deliberate and conscious use of them in order to benefit everything in my life."

Ed may not have consciously known about feng shui, but his

Higher Self provided the intuitive prompting to create beneficial chi.

How to Improve Your Love Chi

Take a relationship inventory of your home by examining the southeast and southwest quarters in every room. Pay special attention to your bedroom.

Implement some of the suggestions provided in this chapter. It may be useful to consult a feng shui guide for a more in-depth treatment. You may even want to bring in a feng shui consultant to make recommendations.

Take a cue from Anne, and place personal objects that have great emotional significance to you in strategic locations throughout your home. And take a cue from Ed, and pay attention to your intuitive promptings. Make the future become a reality by giving it an anchor in physical space.

Clear the clutter

One of the most important improvements you can make in home energy is the removal of physical clutter, which is lethal to good chi. Think of clutter as a form of respiratory congestion: when your lungs are congested, you can't breathe properly, and you don't feel well. You lose energy. When your home is congested with clutter, chi cannot properly flow and energize your space. It becomes stagnant. Thus, clutter hinders your ability to be in top form spiritually.

Piles of old or unread magazines and mail are good candidates for the round file. Clothing that hasn't been worn in a year should be recycled through charity. Boxes of old mementoes can be pared down substantially. Are you a saver, holding on to all sorts of odds and ends just in case you might need them for some unforeseen, future event? Let them go!

Clutter is often hidden from sight, but it's nonetheless detrimental. We might think that putting things away in boxes is a neat way to keep things that we no longer need but don't want to release. However, closets, basements, attics, and garages stuffed with boxes are congested spaces. Their congestion affects the whole environment.

When a friend told Marta that her personal life would shift if she cleaned out her house, Marta scoffed. How could all of her stuff affect her love life? Her friend surveyed her closets and shook her head. "How do you expect anything new to find a place here when you've got every available inch stacked to the max?" she said.

Marta reluctantly agreed that she could get rid of a few things. With the help of her friend, she started clearing out the house. She had to admit that she'd forgotten the contents of many of her storage boxes. "If you don't know you have it, you can't use it, and it's not doing you any good," said her friend. "These things hold the energy of the past. They get in the way of the present and the future."

It took a lot of willpower, but Marta was able to release many things. She saved those items that had the strongest personal meaning to her. When the job was done, she had to admit that her place had a different feel. It seemed lighter and more open, as though fresh air had come through.

Marta began to visualize her home as a place receptive to

new energy and specifically a new relationship. In a strange way, she felt reenergized herself. Was it just a coincidence that soon thereafter her goal came into manifestation? Changes in energy—which affect our thoughts, visioning, and intuition—have to happen first before we can bring change into the material world. Marta took other actions to manifest her soulmate dream, but clearing her house was an important factor. "I think one of the most significant effects of the cleaning was in me," she said. "It's like when you go out and buy a new outfit and you know you look great in it. It changes your whole confidence and behavior."

When your home breathes freely, so do you. You breathe in deeply the breath of Spirit, the breath of God.

Love and blessings

Above all, love your home. Love it even if it is temporary. You cannot expect love to come and stay in a place that is unloved. A place that is loved for being home will invite more love in.

I recommend doing home blessings as part of your home maintenance. You clean your home physically by dusting, vacuuming, straightening, washing, and doing repairs. A home blessing cleans the energy environment and enhances the chi. The chi is affected not only by environmental factors but also by the energies of everyone who comes to a place. A periodic blessing regenerates the spirit of a home and makes it sparkle with an inviting warmth.

Home blessings should be done in new homes after you've

moved in and settled your belongings. Home blessings should be done in existing homes every few months to keep the energy fresh, especially if you are actively seeking a new romantic partnership. I also recommend home blessings to mark the changing of the seasons: the equinoxes, or March 21–22 and September 21–22, and the solstices, or June 21–22 and December 21–22. Home blessings also can be done any time there is a major change, such as a renovation, or to mark a personal turning point.

The blessing is a simple ceremony. You can adopt the following formula to suit your own needs. To be effective, a blessing ceremony should come alive with your own creativity.

Start by focusing your intent. You will offer a prayer as part of your blessing. Compose a prayer. It should include thanks for the home itself, for the sanctuary, protection, and comfort that it provides. If you are seeking a partner, ask for the one who is right for you to share your home with you. If you have a partner and wish to strengthen the bond, ask for the home to help love grow. Include in the prayer any other special purposes, such as turning points, transitions, and changes of the seasons. Keep the prayer simple and short. You will be repeating it several times, and it will be easier for you to put a lot of energy into it if it is short. Some examples of home blessing prayers are at the end of this chapter.

Collect items to represent the four elements, such as a small dish of water; a stone, crystal, or dish of salt for earth; a feather or incense for air; and a candle for fire.

Place the representatives of the elements on your altar. You can add anything else that feels appropriate, such as a small plant or personal items, especially something that signifies soulmate to you. A pair of items reinforces partnership. Balance cool and warm colors. For candles, I always use white for home blessings. White symbolizes purity.

Conduct the home blessing when you have plenty of time. After the blessing, it is good to relax and let the energy of the blessing settle in.

When you are ready to begin, set up your altar in the living room of the house, which is the main room that is fed by all other rooms.

Light your candle (and incense if you've chosen that) and open your ceremony with your prayer. Put as much emotional intensity into it as possible. Visualize what you are praying for with as much vivid detail as possible. *Feel* the prayer as reality, now.

Take the candle and walk from room to room. In every room, say your prayer.

When you are done making a circuit of the house, return to the living room. Place your candle back on the altar. End with a closing prayer, for example: "I give thanks for the sanctuary of this beautiful home, and for the blessings of love and prosperity that flow here."

If you love your home, your home will love you back. Like a mirror, it will reflect the emotions you offer it. This vibration of love will have a noticeable effect on others. Intuitively sensitive people will have a conscious reaction, and others will react unconsciously. They will like and love your home.

Here are examples of home blessing prayers. Copy them into a little notebook and compose your own.

Prayer for Love

May this house be the center of love;
May this house be the center of joy;
May this house nourish and protect.
May new love come and flourish here.
For these and other blessings, I give thanks.

Prayer for Sanctuary

Dear Creator, look graciously upon this home.
Give all who come here wisdom, strength, love, and peace.
Fill this home with happiness.
Make this home a sanctuary, a place of safety and comfort.

Uganda Prayer for General Home Blessing

Let me smile in good fortune;
Let my loved ones smile in good fortune;
Let my home smile in good fortune.
I am always smiling in good fortune.

Omaha Indian Prayer for General Home Blessing

May the house wherein I dwell be blessed;
May good thoughts here possess me;
May my path of life be straight and true;
My dreams as here I lie be joyous;
All above, below, about me
May the house I love be hallowed.

Finally, I'd like to share a prayer composed by my husband, Tom. It's longer than the previous home blessings but is a fitting prayer, especially for the closing of a blessing ceremony.

TOM WRIGHT'S PRAYER FOR HOME HAPPINESS

God of I AM, with the thought that I must lift myself up, I pray for the all-encompassing, outwardly reaching Joy contained in Love. Not your Love for me, My God, in which I implicitly trust, but your Love in me overflowing and manifesting from me. May I be a cocreator with you, My God. May I touch and hold and cherish what I was once too ignorant to see. And let me remember, My God, that of all the people to whom kindness should be shown, I pray that I share the best with my loved ones. I pray that when lessons to learn burn the soul, that cooling patience, unshakable Love, and ultimate trust play their parts. I pray for faith that the kingdom of heaven manifest in my being and that my actions being guided by my ideals be really You in disguise. I pray for the wisdom to know the path, to feel the path, to share the path with my wife [spouse or partner], my family, and my friends. So Be It Now, My God, Your Love within me free.

16

Your Higher Purpose

This is the true joy in life, the being used for a purpose recognized by yourself as a mighty one.

—GEORGE BERNARD SHAW

Soulmates come together for each other: to offer a love and companionship. Soulmate relationships have a feeling of completeness. Many feel it is something they've earned or for which they have waited a long time.

Soulmates also have a sense that they were brought together for a higher purpose. They have a sense of destiny that goes beyond the personal. The support, trust, and love of a soulmate relationship creates space for freedom. Each partner is liberated to explore his or her true self, without worry or fear of how the other partner is going to respond. Soulmates do not have to conform to expectations. This liberation releases a tremendous creative energy, which can be explored individually and together.

Marian, a writer, said:

I didn't realize how emotionally closed off I was until I met Tod. I thought I was being creative, but in truth I wasn't reaching down into my depths. When I look at my old writing, I can see how superficial I was.

After we got together, I began experiencing enormous surges of creative energy. I was inspired to write in a way I never had before. I was astonished at what flowed out of me. I even wrote *poetry,* something that wouldn't have appealed to me before.

I think Tod helped me lose a lot of fear. I wasn't afraid to go inside anymore. I didn't have to fear whether or not I found acceptance. I began to understand what it truly means to be an *artist.*

I asked Marian if she thought she would have reached these inner depths on her own at some point in her career. She said:

I think that's a what-if that's hard to answer. Perhaps so, but I have this feeling in the bottom of my heart that Tod has enabled me to find myself, not just as an artist, but as a person. Loving him has opened up an emotional vulnerability and depth in me that I had not experienced before. Our relationship is so complete and supportive that it feels almost effortless. The relationships that I had before sucked up a lot of energy. You know: "Why does he do this, why doesn't he do that, what will happen if I do this." When doubts and fear take up your energy, you don't have it for other things. This relationship doesn't take energy —it *gives* energy.

We often spend a lot of energy and time in relationships trying to change the other person's behavior to suit our expectations. We play the If Only game: "If only he/she would . . . then I would be happy."

Soulmates don't try to change their partners. They don't need to, for they accept their partners as they are. Instead, they help their partner bring out their best. The help may be in the form of specific action taken, but often is simply woven into the fabric of the relationship itself.

Roger said:

> I sum it all up by saying I'm just plain lucky. I'm lucky to have found my soulmate, and I feel lucky all the time now. Things go right in ways they didn't before. I'm always getting the lucky breaks.

The feeling of luck is a change of consciousness that affects the forces of manifestation. People who feel lucky radiate an optimism and expectation that everything in life is going well for them. This mind-set magnetizes desired outcomes, which manifest as lucky breaks. The feeling of being lucky comes from the liberation that a soulmate relationship provides.

Beyond the harmony of daily life lies a deeper sense of the purpose of a soulmate relationship. Many soulmates feel they joined together specifically to do certain partnership work in the world, especially of a spiritual or humanitarian nature. As Paul Robear said of his relationship with Laura Lee:

> We feel that God didn't give us each other just to enjoy each other but to do specific spiritual work together. We complement each other. We have more power to get our job done together than separately.

Craig and Sandy M. became charity activists. The charity work, done in their free time, "is one way we can put the love we share out into the world," said Sandy.

For many couples, their children are part of their spiritual purpose. Said Lisa:

> I think there are many reasons why David and I are together, but both of us feel very strongly that we are meant to bring certain souls into the world. We have a contract, an agreement that we made with these souls before coming into this life. This is the time for the Children of Light. Enlightened souls are incarnating to help with the advancement of the world.

The higher purpose of a soulmate relationship also can take on a more mystical dimension. Said Lori of her relationship with Bill:

> Our relationship takes us into the unknown. I see the Divine in Bill, and he sees it in me. Together we have a oneness that feels at one with all of creation. We are so connected that we often know each other's thoughts—we *feel* each other's thoughts. We are inseparable, even if we are far apart geographically. But it's more than just a connection between the two of us. We feel bonded to everything that is. While I know that every person really is part of everything, I don't have quite the same feeling by myself. It's as though our partnership magnifies something, takes it to another level.

The mystical depths of a relationship are especially experienced during sex. Many soulmates describe the passionate side of their relationship as sacred. The physical union of the masculine and feminine has always been magical and mystical; it is the creative force of life itself. Rituals symbolizing the marriage of heaven and earth have been recorded since antiquity. Mystical literature of the East and West has used erotic terms and images to describe the union of the human soul with God. The act of sex represents a oneness of being that is not achieved through any other form of communing.

The drive for sexual satisfaction and procreation is powered at the level of the lower chakras. In a more spiritualized union, sexual energy and fulfilment raise consciousness to the higher chakras of enlightenment. One woman described:

> Our sex is more of a sacrament than just a physical act. It's more than a whole-body experience—it's a whole-being experience. I feel we are united in both body and soul, and that in the expression of our lovemaking we touch God. I completely lose a sense of my physical self. We merge into the All. It's an incredible peace and bliss.

Exploring Your Higher Purpose

When you find your soulmate, you may quickly get an intuitive understanding of a higher purpose to your relationship. The higher purpose also will reveal itself as the relationship matures. It is likely to have many dimensions and not be single-purpose in nature.

You can explore your higher purpose and gain greater insight into it by undertaking some activities. It is best to do them together.

Meditation and prayer

Spend time every day meditating or praying together. Ask to be shown what you are meant to do together. Sit quietly and allow information to be revealed to you. Do not worry if little seems to come, especially initially. Meditation and prayer change consciousness. When you do these activities together, you join your consciousnesses to a common goal. You may receive the same insights simultaneously, or each of you may receive insights and inspirations on your own.

Dreamwork

Before retiring, do a dream incubation. Ask for your dreams to reveal the purpose of your relationship or the work you are meant to do together.

Sacred sex

Turn some of your sexual encounters into sacred rituals. Meditate together beforehand on union of body, mind, and soul.

Past-life recall

Many soulmates feel they have shared previous lives, and they gain greater insights into their life paths by undertaking past-life recall. You might attend a group regression, in which a facilitator regresses a large group of people by using light hypnosis or suggestion. The group may be taken to a specific period or a specific lifetime, or given the suggestion to see a meaningful life.

Private regression sessions for individuals or couples also are offered by many facilitators.

Some facilitators are psychologists and counselors, and others are trained hypnotists. I have undertaken past-life recall in group and individual settings by both types of facilitators and have had satisfactory experiences. Check the credentials and experience of the leader before you do sessions. Past-life recall can bring highly emotional material to the surface.

Create a vision

Discuss and write down ideas you each have about your relationship. Be spontaneous to allow the intuition to function. When you have a mutual *aha!* explore those ideas further. Use them as seeds for meditation, prayer, and dreamwork.

Your higher purpose together can take many forms. It may be supporting each other's dreams. It may be building a family. It may be joining forces for a specific work partnership. Allow your higher purpose to manifest in whatever way the relationship needs. Allow it to unfold and grow as both of you change and grow.

17

When You Are Apart

Two souls with but a single thought
Two hearts that beat as one.

—FRIEDRICH HALM

Few couples can be like Paul and Linda McCartney, who were separated for only nine days of their twenty-nine years together. For most of us, the demands of jobs and family require separations. We also have our own interests and pastimes to pursue that may not involve our partners. Soulmates appreciate that each partner needs space. However, soulmate couples dislike separations, especially long ones. They will often go to great lengths to stay in touch.

Said Glenda:

When I was married before, I often looked forward to my husband going away on business trips. It was like a relief to have the house to myself. I didn't need to hear from him daily. I didn't realize for a long time what this was telling me about the state of intimacy in our relationship.

Now that I am with my soulmate, things are much different. We have a strong desire and even a need to communicate whenever we are apart. Unless the logistics are absolutely prohibitive, we have a phone conversation every night, even if it is just to say good night and I love you. We also use E-mail a lot, but calling is best. There is something about hearing the sound of each other's voice that eases the separation. We have been together for ten years, and our desire to talk to each other has never lessened. Both of us have to travel for work, and we will always try to arrange our itineraries to minimize the time away from each other.

Whether or not you are able to stay in touch by telephone and E-mail, try meditating together at an appointed time, if schedules and time zones permit. Carry photos of each other and use the photos to focus your intent. If you are not able to meditate together, meditate on your partner prior to retiring. Visualize the two of you connected at the heart by a cord of light. Surround your partner in radiance of light, and send thoughts of love and protection. Send your partner a kiss.

Said Mary:

I always meditate on my partner whenever he is away. I do it right before I go to bed, so it is the last thing on my mind before I go to sleep. Sometimes one or both of us will have vivid dreams of being together that night.

For author Nathaniel Hawthorne, dusk was the most potent time of connection. He wrote to his wife, Sophia, during one of his travels and told her:

I invite your spirit to be with me,—at any hour and as many hours
as you please,— but especially at the twilight hour, before I light
my lamp. I bid you at that particular time, because I can see visions more vividly in the dusky glow of firelight than either by day-
light or lamplight.

The diffuse light of dusk can be imitated by dim and diffuse
lighting in a room. When light is dim, the eyes tire of trying to
see things clearly. It then becomes easier to shift awareness in-
ward, to perceive things with the inner eye while staying mentally alert. You may not see actual visions such as described by
Hawthorne, but you may have a strong sense of presence with
your loved one.

Dreams and OBEs

Some couples use dreams as a way of staying in touch long distance. Use incubation to invite dreams about, or with, your
distant soulmate: "Tonight I will dream about _____" or
"tonight _____ and I will share a dream with each other." The
more the two of you practice this, the more likely you will have
mutual dream encounters. You may even have lucid dreams in
which you know you are dreaming during the dream. You may
experience a combination of dreams and visions.

Lucid dreams are often erotic in nature. Studies of lucid
dreaming show that women are more likely to have intense sexual feelings and orgasms in lucid dreams than men. Dream sex,
like real sex, is marked by physiological responses in the body.

According to dream researcher Stephen LaBerge, "In some respects, lucid dream sex has as powerful an impact on the dreamer's body as the real thing."

Mary, who described her vivid dreams above, noted that many of these dreams are lucid and involve romantic and erotic encounters with her soulmate.

Dream incubation may also enable you to have an out-of-body experience in your dreams, in which you have the vivid sensation of actually being in a distant location. You may suddenly find yourself there, or you may have a sensation of leaving your physical body and transporting yourself, or flying, to your soulmate.

One of the most unusual cases on record of long-distance contact involving dreams and a possible OBE occurred in 1863. Anxiety over safety was the driving emotional force behind it.

S. R. Wilmot, a manufacturer who lived in Bridgeport, Connecticut, set sail from Liverpool, England, to New York on the steamer *City of Limerick* on October 3, 1863. He shared a stern berth with an Englishman, William J. Tait. On the second day out, a severe storm arose at sea, lasting for nine days and causing damage to the ship. Wilmot experienced seasickness and remained in his berth for several days.

On the night following the eighth day of the storm, the winds and sea abated, and Wilmot was at last able to fall into a much-needed sleep. Toward morning, he dreamed he saw his wife come to the door of the stateroom, clad in her white nightdress. At the door, she noticed that Wilmot was not alone in the room, and she hesitated. Then she entered, came to Wilmot's side, bent down, kissed and caressed him, and then quietly left.

When Wilmot awoke, he was startled to see Tait staring down

at him from his upper berth, which was off to one side and not directly above Wilmot. Tait chided him for having a lady come and visit him during the night. Tait said he had been awake when he saw a woman in a white nightdress enter the stateroom and kiss and caress the sleeping Wilmot. His description exactly matched Wilmot's dream.

When Wilmot returned home to Connecticut, his wife asked if Wilmot had received a visit from her on the night he had the dream. When she heard the reports of the storm, she had become very worried about his safety, especially when she learned that another ship, the *Africa,* had run aground in the same storm and had been forced to shore at Saint John's, Newfoundland, with serious damage.

On the night that Wilmot was able to sleep, Mrs. Wilmot lay awake in bed for a long time thinking about her husband. At about four o'clock in the morning, it seemed to her that she actually went out to search for him. She crossed the stormy sea until she came to a long, black steamship. She went up the side, descended into the cabin, passed through to the stern, and proceeded until she found Wilmot's stateroom. She described the room accurately to Wilmot and said that when she came to the doorway, she saw a man in the upper berth intently watching her. For a moment she was frightened to go in. She decided to enter, and went to Wilmot's side, where she kissed and caressed him and then went away.

When she awoke in the morning, Mrs. Wilmot told her mother about the experience, which seemed to have been a dream, yet was so vivid that Mrs. Wilmot could not shake the feeling that she had physically visited her husband aboard the ship.

Psychical researchers who investigated this intriguing incident opined that a telepathic link might have occurred and taken the form of dreams. In my opinion, I think that Mrs. Wilmot's intense emotional state as she went into sleep facilitated an out-of-body experience during dreaming, which is why it seemed so vivid and real to her—and why Tait, who was not asleep and dreaming, was able to see her as though she were really present.

Intensity

The key to this and other dramatic forms of nonphysical connection is intensity of emotion. Project your consciousness as much as possible. If you cannot envision the environment around your soulmate, connect to him or her by the senses. Imagine the two of you touching and speaking. Feel clothing and skin. Smell hair, skin, and the scents your soulmate may wear.

Consciousness travels in different ways, and these can vary according to the individual, emotions, and circumstances. You may not experience the dramatic effect of leaving your physical body behind, but you may have an equally dramatic experience of being present with your love, while you are still aware of your own surroundings.

18

Rainbows and Angels

*Love is a mystery that transforms everything it touches
into things beautiful and pleasing to God.*

—Saint Faustina Kowalska

Do angels orchestrate the circumstances that bring soulmates together? I believe that God's messengers do help us with
our heart's desires.

One of the deepest soulmate connections I ever witnessed
was between Ray and Kathleen. Soon after I got to know them,
they shared their story with me, and their belief that angels had
played a major role in their relationship.

Coming together in midlife, they asked each other the questions that others in similar circumstances ask: "Where were you
years ago? Why didn't I meet you first and avoid all the pain I
went through in those other relationships?"

We can only trust that we are guided to meet others when
the time is right. Perhaps we need to have certain experiences
first so that we are prepared for the relationship we truly desire
and are ready to have.

Prior to their meeting, Kathleen had reached the lowest point of her life. She had struggled to survive for twenty-seven years in a destructive marriage that took a heavy emotional toll. With two children at home, she felt trapped. She had nowhere to turn for support, nowhere to go. Kathleen said:

I was married to a dominating man. I fought for equality in my marriage and never was able to achieve it. The lack of equality and respect destroyed the very foundation of our relationship. I can't believe I'm part of that cliché about people staying together for their kids, but that's what I did. I stayed when the pain for myself was awful. I couldn't dissociate from it. Until I literally left my home, I could not understand the incredible emotional bind that I was in. My husband had a hold of my heart, and I couldn't see it until I got out of it. I didn't understand that the things he was doing and saying to me were abuse. One of the most damaging things about my marriage was that I could not share my soul. If you can't share your soul, then you're only acting out an existence rather than truly living.

I felt increasingly paralyzed. I had become more introspective. I had a sense of hopelessness, a lack of a future. I felt deep inadequacies about myself, that I was never going to be good enough, that I was never going to find something creative in life, that past talents were dead or didn't amount to anything. I had a feeling that I had no power in my life, that I was crippled, that I couldn't make a difference. No matter what I did in my marriage, nothing changed. I was dead-ended. An image that came to me of my marriage was of a long hallway, and all the doors were shut. Nothing was at the end.

The notion that God might help didn't occur to Kathleen. "It was my theory that there is a Creator, but he does not put his finger into our lives," she said. "That would trivialize him. People who thought their lives were so important that their prayers would be answered—well, I thought that was a fallacy."

In agony over her marriage, Kathleen sought help with various individuals. One was a minister. Once, while talking with her, Kathleen had an extraordinary experience. Suddenly she felt a presence that was like a light streaming toward her. It was so profound that she began shaking. The minister told her it was a sign, a facilitator, a signal. But even though she knew she had to take action to alleviate her pain, Kathleen could not yet summon her resolve. She was like thousands of others who find themselves trapped in desperate circumstances—afraid that letting go of one bad situation would only bring a worse one in.

Meanwhile, in another state hundreds of miles away, Ray was living a life that was not dire, but it was stagnant emotionally and spiritually.

"I was never happy in my marriage," Ray said. "I was emotionally hungry, and I didn't find what I was looking for. My wife and I started drifting apart the same year we were married. But we kept things going on an even keel—we had three beautiful boys."

Ray eventually moved out and went to work in another state. He and his wife remained married, but they lived completely separate lives. Ray had other relationships, but none worked out for the long term. He said:

I've always been searching for that relationship that most of us know in our hearts must exist," he said. "But we tend to take second best, because that is what we find there on the plate. We don't think to keep looking for the best. People look at what comes along, at what's been given to them on their plate and say, well, this doesn't look bad, it isn't exactly what I ordered, but I'll eat it, anyway. But what they're waiting for is that plate that blows everything else out of the water and is just sugar plums and angel dust. That's what you've got to hold out for. If you get sidetracked, you waste years looking for that love you really want.

So, I was keeping very busy with work, but I was very empty in one part—I had no one to share my love of nature with, my love of writing with. I had fame and money, but they don't count. I wanted more than that.

Ray and Kathleen met in what seemed like serendipity at a conference. Initially, nothing happened. But they met again the following year at the same annual conference. One day at lunchtime, Kathleen approached Ray and said, "What are you doing later this afternoon? I'm going to be taking that boat trip up the river."

Ray looked at her and said matter-of-factly, "What am I going to be doing this afternoon? I'm going to be lifting weights."

Kathleen persevered. "What are you going to be doing later on tonight?"

Ray then gave an answer that surprised him: "I'm going to be in the lobby at seven-thirty, and I'd like to take you to dinner." Kathleen smiled.

"We went to dinner at a place where we'd been before, where most of the people from the conference were going," said Ray. "We sat across from each other, and I never looked at anything else but Kathleen the whole time. All I looked at was her beautiful face. I never took my eyes off her face, and she never took her eyes off of me. We talked, and as we talked, we fell in love in a way that I thought was not possible. I never thought that anything like that would happen to me. I thought she was charming, intelligent, lovely, and so beautiful, not just her exterior but in her soul as well."

They went to their separate rooms that night, but neither one could sleep all night long. "I felt something was moving my life," Kathleen said. "All I could think of was love. We had discussed writing to each other, and it was such a remarkable coincidence that both of us wanted to write to another person and have it be meaningful—neither of us had had that experience. We started writing to each other, and this has promoted and enhanced our love right from the beginning. When I write to Ray, it is as if I open my soul and pour it out to him."

They met again two months later and consummated their love. "The first time we made love, even though we knew what sex was all about, we knew that this was something different from anything we had ever experienced in our lives before," said Ray. "Everything we knew about sex meant absolutely nothing. It was as if a door had opened. This was the very first time that both of us had made love. This is a completely new game. It's transcended everything I've ever known about this world. We've been guided by angels and loving spirits who want us to experience the vitality of love such as very few humans are privileged to experience."

For Kathleen, it marked a dramatic turning point.

I was suddenly awakened to incredible needs in myself. Needs that hadn't been met by my destructive marriage. It was the greatest pain in my life to make that decision to leave my marriage, but I was finally able to say that I deserved to be happy. I saw that I was staying in the marriage out of fear, and that scared me. I could not go on living the way I was living, because that would be a lie. I could not face the rest of my life living as though I were in prison. So I chose life rather than death. The other way, I was definitely dying.

Ray told me, "Life is very full, Kathleen." Suddenly I was hearing the most refreshing, wonderful thing. I was excited by it. It set off bells in my head. I knew intuitively that I was with somebody who was not going to take from me. The relationship I'd been in was annihilating me. I didn't have anything more to give. Ray has never taken—he helps me to give more.

Ray and Kathleen began a courtship while they sorted out their personal and professional lives. There were daily phone calls, frequent letters, and frequent visits. They both felt that angels had had a hand in bringing them together.

Lovemaking was often accompanied by a sense of a great aura of loving energy around them. In addition, Kathleen began having spontaneous visions of beautiful nature scenes, such as sunsets, tropical flowers, or of tropical birds, all in brilliant and vibrant colors that were alive with energy, unlike anything she has ever seen on earth. The visions were a sign to her that she and Ray were meant to be together.

One vision was astonishing in its direct link to him. It happened on a weekend that we had been together. It was in the morning. Ray had gotten up and had taken a shower. I wasn't really asleep. I had my eyes closed. He came to the bed and reached out his hand and touched me. I saw this vision where he touched me, and it was mauve roses coming at me. I opened my eyes, and he said, "You will let me take care of you, won't you?" I said, "Of course." Then I had an incredible need to shut my eyes again, that there was something unfinished. I shut my eyes and saw a bouquet of mauve roses coming at me. I associated the flowers with his care for me.

Kathleen said her visions were not fleeting but lingered for a long time. She had the ability to leave them and reenter them. They were vivid and not dreamlike. One vision came while they were in a park, leaning up against a tree, kissing and caressing very sensuously. With her eyes closed, Kathleen saw a magnificent vision of deep purple blue mountains against a sunset of violent orange. Two days later, on a trip into the mountains, she was amazed to see a sunset similar to the one in her vision. Another time, one evening after making love, she saw a surrealistic, swirling ribbon of many colors. "It seemed to represent the emotional, physical side of our love," she said.

The visions and the auras created a transcendent sense that they were deeply connected beyond the physical, in a state of being without form, eternal, filling the universe with a golden light of love. Said Ray:

It's beautiful. Nothing else matters. I love her totally and completely, with all my heart and with all my soul, forever and ever. This is another one of the gifts that has been given to us by the angels. The love that Kathleen and I have is worth more than all the gold in the world. Money, gold, silver, jewels, possessions don't

224 Heart & Soul

matter. Once you're in love, everything suddenly comes into perspective.

I think angels can precipitously change people's lives, and they choose people for that very carefully. I think they chose us to be brought together. They worked everything out so we were in the right jobs at the right time at the right place. Then they took hold of both of us and shook us and said, *Wake up!*

There had to be another hand in it. I don't know whose. A strong, loving hand had to bring our life lines together and guide us from that time on. The angels are the instruments of that hand, and they are always with us. When we part, the angels cry, as we do. The angels are extremely happy when we meet. They're holding us together. I don't see angels as entities but as something very powerful that interacts in our lives in the most benevolent ways, to give Kathleen especially some very beautiful insight into the spirit world through her visions. They've enabled me to say and do things that I don't know where they've come from.

I've never wanted anything from Kathleen, I've never demanded anything, never pressed her for anything. That has been reinforced by the angels—that I am to love her, serve her, protect her. Our love is a precious flower beyond all expectations. We have a love that literally knows no bounds. At times, when we experience this fourth dimension, our love is really expanded beyond the limits of the known universe.

After a long-distance courtship of nearly two years, Ray and Kathleen at last were able to marry. They settled into the perfect country house. But six months later, a few days before Christmas, a heart attack took Ray away. He died in Kathleen's arms. Love does not end at the grave. Soulmates, who understand how the deep connection between them spans beyond the present life, know well that death does not diminish love. The enormous grief of being separated in physical life is eased over time with repeated signs that the soul-to-soul bond remains strong.

When I asked Kathleen for permission to revisit their love story, it was like being a messenger from heaven. Kathleen explained that through various events, it seemed as though Ray were sending a love message to her.

She recalled of their relationship:

> My memories are of a very unique time and love. I was completely in love with Ray and I believe, he with me. The wonderful and frequent visions were also unique and marvelously vibrant. When we lived together those short two years before we were married, we were unbelievably contented and harmonious. I am, of course, saddened when I think how abruptly our married life was ended.

Ray had been interested in alchemy and the tarot, and I had given him a set of *The Alchemical Tarot* book and cards, which I coauthored with Robert Michael Place. The tarot is an excellent tool for meditation, dreamwork, and intuition development, and alchemical images pertain especially to spiritual awakening and enlightenment.

Kathleen told me:

> After Ray died, I took out your tarot cards that you gave Ray as a gift. I have a girlfriend who showed me how to read them based upon a formula she brought to me. According to one of the central cards, the High Priestess, a person would take me to the door of my future—but not go through with me.

I thought this was uncannily true. Several incidents after Ray's death made me believe he was reaching back through time. One day, during the month of our birthdays, September—the year after he died—I accidentally activated an old tape that was still on the telephone. There was a message from Ray to me that I had never received, telling me how much he loved me and that he could not wait until I came home.

Kathy and Ray are still united but in a different way and across different worlds. They will come home together again, somewhere else, in some other time.

19

Calling in Your Soulmate

*He calls all things that are not and by his calling
makes them exist.*

—Romans 4:17

Now you know how to manifest. It's time to act. Call in
your soulmate. Make a divine appointment with you and your
lover. Visualize it. Pray it. Affirm it. Demand it!

Have you ever witnessed a faith healing or an evangelical
gathering? Intense energy is raised by calling in whatever is desired as though it already exists. There isn't a shred of doubt. The
people involved have an all-consuming belief and faith in the
delivery of what they want. They have the ability to reach into
the unmanifest, the future, and pull their goal into the present.
They don't just ask God for help, they insist and demand in the
name of God. They shout it. They put their bodies in motion.
With the help of God, nothing can be denied them.

The same principles apply to manifestation. You may go
about it metaphysically, philosophically, or religiously, but the
fundamental energy raised is the same. You must *believe* in every
cell of your being that the right person exists for you and *will*

manifest in your life. You must have *faith* that the two of you will be guided to meet. You must affirm that this is in accordance with the right and perfect laws of God or of the universe.

Every day you must call in your soulmate. When you go to work, call in your soulmate. When you do your shopping, call in your soulmate. When you stand in a line, call in your soulmate. Do it silently: *I call in my soulmate now!* When possible, do it out loud. Shout it. Gesture. You must stoke the fires of your intensity so that they always burn, even when you must turn your attention to other things.

Enlist the help of group consciousness. Ask friends to affirm for you. Call prayer chains. Muster all the energy you can on your behalf. *Believe* that the right relationship is here *now*. Keep affirming *now*.

Here is one version of a calling-in.

At first I prayed and meditated while in a sitting position, but I found that wasn't enough. As the energy inside me built up, I wanted to be in motion. I created this ritual. I put on some drumming music and started to move around to it in a circle. I chanted my prayer and affirmation. As I kept moving around the circle, I got more and more energetic, until I was shouting at the top of my voice. The more I put into it, the more I could feel the certainty of success—meeting my soulmate. I ended it by shouting, "I have it *now!*" I would then let the energy settle back down by meditating again and giving thanks for the results I knew I was going to get.

It works. I have recommended to some of my girlfriends that they try it, too.

As mentioned earlier, effective rituals engage the senses and involve some form of kinetic activity. When we put our entire being into manifestation, we become more powerful manifestors. An energetic ritual activates the universal life force energy within us and makes transformation possible. It also strengthens our faith, confidence, and resolve.

Focus on Beauty

When we call in our soulmate, we are seeking a higher vibration of love. The more you elevate your consciousness in other ways, the more you will be attuned to attract this higher love.

Appreciation of beauty is an attunement to heaven, a closeness to God. "For beauty is never without truth, nor truth without beauty," said Saint Francis de Sales.

The beauty of nature is especially conducive to elevation of consciousness. Nathaniel Hawthorne was always aware of the link between beauty and love, and he often commented on beauty in his love letters to his soulmate wife, Sophia. His appreciation of the beauty around him helped him to stay emotionally close to her whenever they were separated.

"What a beautiful day! And I had double enjoyment of it— for your sake and my own," he wrote to her in 1839. "I have been to walk, this afternoon, to Bunker's Hill and the Navy Yard, and am tired, because I had not your arm to support me."

In another letter the same year, Hawthorne wrote, "My definition of Beauty is, that it is love, and therefore includes both truth and good. But only those who love as we do can feel the significance and force of this. . . . I am full of the glory of the day."

Increase your daily awareness of the beauty around you: in nature, in art, in man-made society, in people, in yourself. Beauty expands the heart, increases joy, and raises thoughts. Before you start your day, visualize that it will be happy, harmonious, and beauty-filled. Affirm that you are a channel of love, and that divine love flows to you and through you out into the world. If we are to attract and enjoy the highest earthly love, we must be filled with an abundance of love: love for self, all life, and God.

20

The Soul Magic of Love Letters

So is a word better than a gift.

—ECCLESIASTICUS 18:16

"In a man's letters . . . his soul lies naked," Samuel Johnson, the famous eighteenth-century lexicographer and author, once wrote to his lover, Mrs. Theater. "His letters are only the mirror of his heart."

Ever since men and women first began to commit thought and sentiment to paper, the love letter has served as one of the strongest connections between souls. Lovers have celebrated their joy and lamented their anguish in letters to one another, expressing their deepest feelings, which perhaps they never would have found the courage to speak aloud.

The written word is a wonderful medium for love sentiments. It is intimate and personal; it has the power to conjure up vivid images and feelings. It can be read slowly and savored and reread as often as desired. Unlike soft whispers in the ear, the disembodied voice on the telephone, or the impermanence of cyberspace, the written word lasts, never fading in intensity. Love letters written hundreds of years ago are still fresh and poignant when read today.

Writing love letters is a ritual that binds us to others. A piece of our heart goes into them; we imbue them with our soul essence, making them magical. Every letter is unique, composed on a certain type of paper in a certain ink, expressing certain thoughts that may never be said in quite the same way again. "Something happens to our thoughts and emotions when we put them into letters; they are then not the same as spoken words," says Thomas Moore in *Soul Mates*. "They are placed, in a different, special context, and they speak at a different level, serving the soul's organ of rumination rather than the mind's capacity for understanding."

Letters, of course, were once the only means of communication when face-to-face meetings weren't possible, and so they were written more frequently. It was not uncommon for lovers to write daily or, if a message had only to be delivered across town, even several times a day. Napoleon, in the thick of battles as he conquered his way across the Continent, retired to his tent nearly every night to write his beloved wife, Josephine, a passionate letter. But she didn't feel the same about him, and her lack of reciprocation kept him in a frenzy of worry and jealousy each time they were separated.

Elizabeth Barrett and Robert Browning, whose relationship began with a letter from Robert, wrote to each other often during their crosstown courtship—long letters, sometimes a thousand words or so, filled with sentiments. Robert got right to the point in his first missive with a sincere declaration of love, before they had ever set eyes on each other.

Communicating love is much different today; it is much less

formal. It's often easier to pick up the telephone or buy a card that comes close to expressing your feelings than it is to sit down and compose a message that lays bare your soul. Nevertheless, the love letter endures, because lovers will always need to make some kind of permanent record of their feelings. The love letter actually gets a boost from high technology: the Internet E-mail has rejuvenated letter writing, albeit in a shorthand kind of fashion.

What's in a love letter? Endearments, confessions, one's innermost secret thoughts, descriptions of one's passion. Horatio Nelson, England's greatest naval hero, declared that his lover, Emma Hamilton, was his "Alpha and Omega." Lord Byron, smitten by young Countess Teresa Guiccioli, told her he wished she'd stayed in her convent. "Think of me, sometimes when the Alps and ocean divide us—but they never will, unless you wish it," he wrote her.

The all-time prize for the most profuse and unusual endearments probably goes to Heinrich von Kleist, a German romantic poet who lived around the time of Goethe, in the late eighteenth and early nineteenth centuries. The object of von Kleist's affection was Henrietta Vogel, and one letter to her consisted of nothing but a string of endearments, fifty-nine of them altogether. Besides such typical ones as "my heart-blood," "star of my eyes," and "my all and everything," he came up with "my entrails," "my goods and chattels," "my tragic play," and "my posthumous reputation." In despair over Henrietta's incurable illness, von Kleist committed suicide at age thirty-four, a year after writing that letter. He probably had no idea how much his passion for her influenced his "posthumous reputation."

Love letters also make promises and beg promises. Sir

Richard Steele, an Irish-born English playwright and essayist, beseeched Mary Scurlock to present him with one of her fans, gloves, or masks, "or I cannot live." In wooing Mary, he wrote her, "Methinks I could write a volume to you; but all the language on earth would fail in saying how much and with what disinterested passion I am ever yours."

Some of the most impassioned love letters never reached the hands of the one to whom they were written. After Beethoven died in 1827, three letters were found in his effects. All were addressed to an anonymous "Immortal Beloved" but apparently were never posted. The brilliant composer spent his life as a solitary, moody man, but he poured his heart out in these letters. "Even in bed my ideas yearn toward you," he said. "I can only live, either altogether with you or not at all. . . ." Unfortunately for melancholy Beethoven, it was "not at all." His unsent letters and lack of action thwarted whatever potential existed for magical power.

Letter-writing styles are less flowery today, but love letters still contain our deepest and most sincere thoughts and feelings. Make love letters part of your soulmate connection. You will truly touch the heart of your beloved.

King Charles I of France, who told his wife, Queen Henrietta Maria, that he loved her "above all earthly things," implored her to write to him. He said he desired her "to comfort me as often as thou canst with thy letters. And dost thou not think that to know particulars of thy health, and how thou spendest thy time, are pleasing subjects unto me, though thou hast no other business to write of?"

The Write Art

Here is how to write something straight from your heart.

1. Decide what type of love letter you want to send.

Not all love letters need be eloquent—they can be passionate or even light and humorous. Humor is sometimes the best way to lift spirits and to provide breathing room in a relationship. Select a tone that will best help get your message across and will appeal to your loved one.

Once I was on a radio show talking about how to write love letters. A woman called in and said she had tried twice to impress her lover with love letters, but they hadn't made much impact. She had written out short messages first in French and then in Italian, because she thought they sounded more romantic that way. "Have you tried saying it in English?" I asked. Know your market!

Perhaps you are inspired to write poetry. Lovers love poems. Kathleen often sent her soulmate Ray an inspired poem, such as this one, which was a Valentine gift:

> *My sweet, sweet love*
> *Resplendent with aromatic spices and azure skies*
> *Of golden kisses ripe with the sun's rich glow*
> *The warmth of a rosy aura*
> *Holds our souls in rapture*
> *Folds us in a rich velvet cocoon.*
> *Your presence strikes the hidden pulse*

In my throat and sets myself on fire.
In the warm enclosure of your arms
I unfold like the silky petals of the rose,
Caught in the early summer shower
Of crystal beads and honeyed hours.
As I open to your fervent touch
A lute song echoes across the narrowing space
Transfixing us in the love we create.

Don't be bashful about expressing sentiments. Sentimental cards are popular because people like to give and receive them. It's much more meaningful, however, to say what you feel in your own words.

2. Select the appropriate stationery and writing utensil.

The kind of love letter you want to write will determine your tools. For eloquence, perhaps a rich, high-quality parchment paper, a fountain pen, and brown ink would produce the right effect. For humor, stationery printed with a cute drawing or cartoon might be best. Greeting cards, with or without printed messages, can also set the stage. Office supply places sell a wide variety of great printed stationery. You can even design your own on a computer. Whatever you choose, your letter should convey a feeling of special intimacy. Never, never type a love letter!

Stationery lightly scented with your cologne or perfume may conjure up special memories and emotions. It's important not to overdo the fragrance, however, because a strongly scented letter sitting in a mailbox may embarrass rather than please your lover.

3. Set the right mood.

Treat love letter writing like a ritual. Pick an unhurried time of day or night to write. Shut the door and put the phone on the answering machine. Your sentimental reverie should be uninterrupted. To get in a love-letter-writing mood, gaze at photos of your lover. Play the favorite music you share. Recall your happiest and most loving moments together.

4. Be spontaneous.

It may take you a few starts, but once you get going, let your words and feelings flow honestly and spontaneously. If you rework a love letter too much, it will sound stilted. Let your letter be spontaneously you!

5. Research for inspiration.

Go to the library and look up collections of love letters written by famous men and women of history. Styles of expression vary from person to person as well as from era to era, and you will find some particularly to your liking. Let them inspire you to write your own love letters.

6. Send it.

Sometimes words of heartfelt emotion and passion seem embarrassing once they cool. It's only natural; you've got your heart on the line. Honoré de Balzac once commented on this awkwardness in one of the impassioned letters he wrote to Countess Hanska:

> If you knew what emotion seizes me when I throw one of these packets in the [post] box. My soul flies towards you with these papers; I say to them like a crazy man, a thousand things; like a crazy man I think that they go towards you to repeat them to you; it is impossible for me to understand how these papers impregnated by me will be, in eleven days, in your hands. . . .

Fortunately for them both, Balzac kept sending his love letters. Don't wait for second thoughts to sway you into placing your letter in a drawer instead of the mailbox. Don't be like Beethoven, who composed beautiful love letters to his anonymous "Immortal Beloved," but never sent them.

7. *Go beyond love letters.*

While you're writing romantic love letters, try writing love and appreciation letters that let your partner know how much you appreciate small things they've done for you, or the way they've treated you. Remember, love is what holds everything in creation together, so be generous in giving it.

Keepsakes

When you receive love letters, cherish them and save them. "The soul wants to be accorded a reality beyond our own internal ruminations and ideas," says Thomas Moore. "It needs to find a home in objects, and for the soul of intimacy there is no better home than letters of intimate value saved over a lifetime."

Saving love letters in a special place completes the ritual and preserves their energy.

For Further Inquiry

Several of my books provide more information on working with intuition, dreams, miracle mind consciousness, and prayer.

By Rosemary Ellen Guiley:

Breakthrough Intuition: How to Achieve a Life of Abundance by Listening to the Voice Within (2001), Berkley Books

Dreamspeak: How to Understand the Messages in Your Dreams (2001), Berkley Books

Dreamwork for the Soul (1998), Berkley Books

The Encyclopedia of Dreams (1995), Berkley Books

A Miracle in Your Pocket (2001), Thorsons/HarperCollins

Prayer Works (1998), Unity House

Quotes from the saints are from my book *The Quotable Saint* (2002), published by Facts on File.

Home blessing prayers are from my book *Blessings: Prayers for the Home and Family* (1996), published by Pocket Books.

The earlier story of Ray and Kathleen, and Kathleen's poem, appears in my book *Angels of Mercy* (1993), published by Pocket Books.

I invite you to visit my web site, Visionary Living, at www.visionaryliving.com.

In Addition

The comments from Rudolph Steiner in this book can be found in his book *Intuitive Thinking as a Spiritual Path* (1995), published by the Anthroposophic Press. I also recommend Steiner's *How to Know Higher Worlds* (1994), by the same publisher.

I also highly recommend *Everyday Miracles: The Inner Art of Manifestation* (1996) by David Spangler, published by Bantam Books.

Marcia Emery's quotes and full soulmate story appears in *Hot Chocolate for the Mystical Lover* (1999) by Arielle Ford, published by Plume.

Russ Michael's quotes and soulmate story is told in his book *Finding Your Soulmate* (1992), published by Samuel Weiser.

For advice on feng shui, consult *Practical Feng Shui* (1997) by Simon Brown, published by Ward Lock.

For a wonderful collection of love letters written by famous people, consult *Love Letters* (1976), compiled by Antonia Fraser and published by Weidenfeld & Nicolson. A 1995 edition is published by Leopard Books/Random House.

About the Author

Rosemary Ellen Guiley, Ph.D., is the author of more than twenty-five books on spiritual, metaphysical, inspirational, and paranormal topics. She has written on angels, miracles, dreams, intuition, prayer, healing, mystical experience, magic, and more. Her books are published around the world in twelve languages.

Rosemary is president of her own company, Visionary Living, Inc., a provider and publisher of inspirational and metaphysical materials. Her web site, www.visionaryliving.com, is part of the Angelhaven.com community of web sites. She writes columns and articles for magazines and the web and presents lectures and workshops. She is a former member of the board of directors of the Association for the Study of Dreams, and is an honorary fellow of the College of Human Sciences, the professional membership division of the International Institute of Integral Human Sciences in Montreal, a nonprofit affiliate of the United Nations. She lives in Maryland.